I HATE WINTER

BRONTE CREEK PROVINCIAL PARK

I HATE WINTER

A Guide to Winter Outings in Ontario

Sue Lebrecht

The BOSTON
MILLS PRESS

To Lynn

CATALOGING IN PUBLICATION DATA

Lebrecht, Sue, 1962-
I hate winter : a guide to winter outings in Ontario

ISBN 1-55046-318-7

1. Outdoor recreation - Ontario - Guidebooks. 2. Ontario - Guidebooks.
3. Winter sports - Ontario - Guidebooks. I Title.

FC3057.L42 1999   917.1304'4   C99-931860-8   F1057.7.L42 1999

Published in 1999 by
BOSTON MILLS PRESS
132 Main Street
Erin, Ontario N0B 1T0
Tel 519-833-2407
Fax 519-833-2195
e-mail books@bostonmillspress.com
www.bostonmillspress.com

An affiliate of
STODDART PUBLISHING CO. LIMITED
34 Lesmill Road
Toronto, Ontario, Canada
M3B 2T6
Tel 416-445-3333
Fax 416-445-5967
e-mail gdsinc@genpub.com

Distributed in Canada by
GENERAL DISTRIBUTION SERVICES LIMITED
325 Humber College Boulevard
Toronto, Canada M9W 7C3
Orders 1-800-387-0141 Ontario & Quebec
Orders 1-800-387-0172 NW Ontario
& other provinces
Fax 416-213-1917
e-mail customer.service@ccmailgw.genpub.com
EDI Canadian Telebook S1150391

Distributed in the United States by
GENERAL DISTRIBUTION SERVICES INC.
85 River Rock Drive, Suite 202
Buffalo, New York 14207-2170
Toll-free 1-800-805-1083
Toll-free fax 1-800-481-6207
e-mail gdsinc@genpub.com
www.genpub.com
PUBNET 6307949

Design by Mary Firth
Cover design by Gillian Stead
Cover photographs by Sue Lebrecht
Maps by Steve Jackson
Printed in Canada

THE CANADA COUNCIL | LE CONSEIL DES ARTS
FOR THE ARTS | DU CANADA
SINCE 1917 | DEPUIS 1917

We acknowledge for their financial support of our
publishing program the Canada Council, the Ontario Arts
Council, and the Government of Canada through the Book
Publishing Industry Development Program (BPIDP).

PINERY PROVINCIAL PARK

Acknowledgments

Special thanks to Lisa Dost and Dave Hiscox for joining me on many extended research trips, through storm and shine; to Linda Brentnall, who's always game to go for a trek and alpine ski; and to Lynn Kavanagh, my roommate, who has been supportive throughout this project.

Also, thanks to the numerous media relations people at tourism offices, conservation areas and provincial parks who helped me stitch together the fine points.

Contents

North Central 119

East 145

WYE MARSH WILDLIFE CENTRE

Introduction

Sure, we'd all rather be in the Bahamas. But do you really hate winter? Or do you just hate breaking ice from your windshield, shovelling snow from your driveway, and getting cold feet?

There's no denying that winter has a few miserable characteristics. We can gripe and whine about it, staying indoors as much as possible. But for those who are determined to make the most of the season—enjoying playful prospects outside—this book plows the way.

Contrary to its title, *I Hate Winter* is a celebration of the snowy season. In these pages we'll visit the hottest cold spots in Ontario, from Algonquin Park to Niagara Falls, and from Gatineau Park, near Ottawa, to Pinery Provincial Park, near Grand Bend. You'll get acquainted with the best places to cross-country ski, snowshoe, skate, tube, toboggan, hike, dog sled, winter camp and witness nature's spectacles.

Come visit places where chickadees will eat sunflower seeds from your hand, where you can tube down a hill at 80 kph, snap photos of erupting ice volcanoes, or snowshoe to the source of a sulphur spring that never freezes. Where you can cross-country ski at night under a full moon and on lantern-lit trails, witness thousands of swans passing so low you can hear their wings flap, or rent a cabin or yurt on a wilderness trail system.

Featured too are some of Ontario's favourite winter events, including Minden's Dog Sled Derby, Elmira's Maple Syrup Festival, Owen Sound's Festival of Northern Lights and Ottawa's Winterlude. Numerous other events are also highlighted, along with tour operators offering dog sledding, backcountry skiing and winter camping.

Snow- and ice-related activities, naturally, are weather permitting; so call ahead for conditions. Just as naturally, prices—correct at the time of publication—are subject to change. Finally, remember, Mother Nature doesn't spread her frostings equally. If there's no snow in your driveway, there could be a ton of the stuff less than an hour away.

I Hate Winter is more than just a smorgasbord of cool possibilities—it's a source of motivation. In the winter, just getting dressed for the outdoors is an effort—stepping outside is an achievement. But getting somewhere, doing something different, experiencing a great or little white adventure, can be a wonderful sensation. I'm sure this book, put to use, will warm even the frostiest of attitudes towards winter.

Sue Lebrecht
energie@idirect.com

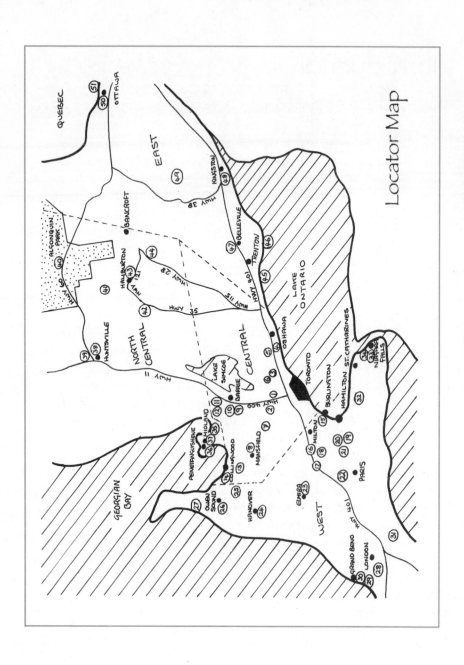

Locator Map

CENTRAL

BLACK CREEK PIONEER VILLAGE

GREATER TORONTO/OSHAWA

 ## 1 *COUNTRY CHRISTMAS,* **BLACK CREEK PIONEER VILLAGE**
Toronto, north end

* wander through a Christmas-decorated 19th-century village
* hear folklore recounted by costumed interpreters
* ride in horse-drawn wagons
* see toy-making demonstrations
* sample traditional food
* eat a four-course Victorian Christmas dinner
* sing carols

When: Mid-Nov to Dec 31, daily, plus Fri and Sat evenings in early Dec
Highlights: The smell of pine boughs, the taste of mulled cider, the glow of lantern-lit streets, the sound of carollers
Impression: Romantic and charming unreality

Magical Misconception

Christmas in the 1860s in rural Upper Canada was quiet. Times were tough and survival was a priority. You'd be lucky to get a present, let alone a roast turkey dinner, stuffed stockings hung by a fireplace and a fully decorated tree. But you won't learn that at Black Creek Pioneer Village. Dressed for a country Christmas, the re-created 19th-century Victorian community, with nearly 40 heritage buildings—including a still-operating, four-storey-high flour mill—presents the prettiest celebration of the past imaginable.

Evergreen garlands and ribbons are strung across buildings, wreaths adorn doors. Carollers sing in the streets, choirs in the church. Two large Christmas trees are decorated in the ballroom of the inn, one with musical ornaments, the other done up in white. Homes are hung with kissing balls and pomanders. Fireplaces are lit, and woodstoves glow. The aromas of fruit cakes, gingerbread, apple schnitz, pies, cookies, mincemeat tarts and plum pudding fill the kitchens. Gifts under trees include scarves, pen wipers and wooden toy tops.

Soulful Authenticity

The scene is almost magical, which isn't to say that Black Creek has lost touch with historical reality. Its Yuletide showcase is authentic early Canadian, following Pennsylvania-German traditions such as the Christmas tree, the Scottish custom of Hogmanay, the Irish crèche and candle in the window, and the foods and decorations of the English. The village presents the way it was, only exaggerated for your romantic pleasure.

Follow dirt roads and wooden plank sidewalks door to door. Visit the blacksmith, enter the post office, wander through a barn, or go to the doctor. See toy-making demonstrations and an impressive 19th-century toy collection. Take a horse-drawn wagon ride along the country roads.

By night, follow the glow of oil lamps, candles and lanterns from home to home. Stop outside for a cup of mulled cider ladled from a large cast-iron pot steaming over a fire, and help yourself to roasted chestnuts. Inside, sit by a fireplace to hear tales told by costumed interpreters, and sample food made the old-fashioned way. Evenings also feature a traditional Christmas dinner of glazed ham and sage-stuffed roast turkey, with all the fixings plus dessert, by reservation only.

GUIDE NOTES

Location
In the north end of Toronto. From Hwy 400, exit at Steeles and drive east just past Jane and follow signs. Accessible by TTC. From the Finch subway, take the Steeles bus 60 B, D or E west.

Open
May 1 to Dec 31. Country Christmas, mid-Nov to Dec 31, 9:30 am to 4 pm, daily. Christmas by Lamplight, Fri and Sat, 6 to 9 pm; reservations required.

Cost
$9 adults, $7 students and seniors, $5 ages 5 to 14, ages 4 and under free. Dinner $30 adults, ages 12 and under half price; advance ticket purchase required.

Facilities
Two gift shops, restaurant with an herb-themed lunch menu, washrooms, coffee cart, vending machines. Visitors' Centre with a display of crèches.

Tips
Evening events sell out early; reserve as early as Aug.

Tourism Info
Tourism Toronto, 800-363-1990 or 416-203-2600, www.tourism-toronto.com.

More Info
Black Creek Pioneer Village, 416-736-1733, www.trca.on.ca.

2   KORTRIGHT CENTRE FOR CONSERVATION
Vaughan

* learn about energy conservation
* learn about sustainable living
* cross-country ski
* bird-watch
* hike nature trails
* participate in numerous outdoor programs
* participate in kids' activity tables and workshops

EVENTS
* Themed programs: Sat and Sun at 11:30 am, 1 pm and 2:30 pm
* Owl Prowl: Two nights, Jan and Feb
* Natural Love Stories: Weekend closest to Valentine's Day
* Maple Syrup Festival: Daily, March to early April

Highlights: Interpretive programs, special events
Impression: An animated, educational immersion into nature and energy conservation

Kortright Centre for Conservation
ROSEMARY HASNER/TRCA

Heightened Awareness

For more than two decades the Kortright Centre for Conservation has been promoting environmental awareness and energy conservation. Wind turbines spin in a high, open field and boardwalks cross lowland marshes. Bird feeders line a forested path. Trails with bridges criss-cross the confluence of the East Humber River and Cold Creek. Posted signs explain special features throughout, and informal educational programs present the wonders of nature and the possibilities for environmentally friendly lifestyles.

Visit on a winter weekend to gaze at snowflakes under magnifiers, identify animal tracks in the snow, learn ice-rescue procedures, or hear the natural history of a variety of wildlife. Kortright Centre for Conservation presents three different programs every Saturday and Sunday—some particularly for children.

On your own, hike the plowed Bird Feeder Trail, a 20-minute-long path through woods dotted with specially designed feeders that provide seeds and fats for various species. An accompanying trail brochure describes the menu at each feeder.

One of three other plowed trails, the Power Trip takes you past electricity-producing windmills and solar panels to an energy-efficient cottage powered entirely by the wind and sun. At the cottage, workshops are offered on subjects such as frugal furnace use, basement renovations, and conservation gadgets. The centre features Canada's most varied display of renewable energy technology. Another building, the Centre for Sustainable Living, serves as a biological waste treatment plant. Essentially, it's a marsh inside a greenhouse.

When snow conditions permit, the centre grooms and tracksets 14 kilometres of cross-country ski trails that roam mature forest and meadows, past frozen marshes and ponds. Parents with young children will also appreciate a small beginner toboggan hill.

The Visitors' Centre is chock-full of permanent and visiting displays, including an exhibit on owl species, aquariums showing how fish live under frozen streams and ponds, and home insulation techniques. The 150-seat theatre features slide presentations and videos. On weekends, youngsters can make pine-cone bird feeders, snowflake cutouts and other crafts at activity centres. Meanwhile, parents huddle around the fireplace in the café, sipping hot chocolate or spooning hearty soup while gazing out the floor-to-ceiling windows—some of which have one-way glass. Outside, a mere arm's length away, birds flit among assorted feeders, unaware they're being watched.

GUIDE NOTES

Location
From Hwy 400, turn west on Major Mackenzie Dr, then south on Pine Valley Dr and go 1 km.

Open
Daily, 10 am to 4 pm.

Cost
$5 adults, $3 children, seniors and students, under 4 free.

Facilities
Main building with exhibits, cafeteria, gift shop, washrooms, theatre.

Events/Programs
Owl Prowl, an evening event, includes an illustrated talk before a hike with naturalists hooting to evoke owl response; reservations required. Natural Love Stories offers a look at how plants have historically been used as aphrodisiacs and love potions. The Maple Syrup Festival features production techniques, pancakes, and horse-drawn wagon rides, and during March Break, there's storytelling for kids, live music, crafts and films.

Tourism Info
Tourism Toronto, 800-363-1990 or 416-203-2600, www.tourism-toronto.com.

More Info
Kortright Centre for Conservation, 905-832-2289, www.kortright.org, Toronto and Region Conservation Authority, 416-661-6600 ext 203, www.trca.on.ca.

Kortright Centre for Conservation
ROSEMARY HASNER/TRCA.

3   CEDARENA
Markham

❄ skate on natural ice

EVENT
🛷 Cedarena Birthday Party: Last Tues in Jan

Highlight: Birthday party with spot prizes, doughnuts and hot chocolate
Impression: Ontario's prettiest skating rink

Ice Ambience
Set in the Rouge Valley, surrounded by large cedars and made all the more romantic with waltzing music, Cedarena is a large, natural-ice rink. It sits at the end of a wooded trail, which leads from a parking lot in a frozen field.

Built and maintained by the hamlet of Cedar Grove, Cedarena first opened in 1927 after local farmers cleared and levelled the area, then pumped up water from the Rouge River for a surface. The rink-side benches have been there for 70 years. The woodstove-heated chalet, decorated with Christmas lights, is original.

Expect a bumpy surface and nostalgia for a time you may have known only in archival photographs.

GUIDE NOTES

Location
From Hwy 401, go north on Hwy 48 (Markham Rd) to Steeles, go east to Reesor Rd and then north 1 km.

Open
Weather dependent; usually the first week of Jan to the first week of March. Thurs, Fri and Sat 7:30 to 10 pm, Sun 1 to 4 pm, adults only Tues 7:30 to 10 pm.

Cost
Thurs to Fri $2 adults, $1 ages 12 and under, Sat to Sun $2.50 adults, $1 children.

Facilities
Heated chalet with washrooms.

Events/Programs
Birthday party $4. Private functions Mon and Wed.

Tourism Info
Information Markham,
905-415-7500,
or York Region Tourism,
888-448-0000,
www.region.york.on.ca.

More Info
Cedarena, 905-294-0038.

4   LYNDE SHORES CONSERVATION AREA
Whitby

❄ hand-feed birds and squirrels
❄ hike trails
❄ dog walk
❄ wander Lake Ontario's shoreline

Highlight: Birds land in your hand
Impression: Animated interaction

Fancy Feeding
Lynde Shores Conservation Area, a home for wintering songbirds and little critters, offers wildlife encounters of the feathered and furry kind. Chickadees land in the palm of your hand and chubby squirrels and chipmunks bound up to greet you.

The highlight of the park is the Bird Feeder Trail, a short loop through the forest. Featuring 20 feeders, plus a couple of suet feeders, it attracts about 10 different species, including cardinals, woodpeckers, mourning doves and nuthatches.

Bring unsalted sunflower seeds and hold them in the flat palm of your hand. In no time, resident chickadees with white faces, dark caps and bibs will be taking turns landing on your hand to pick a treat. A downy woodpecker may also drop in, and dozens of squirrels hope for handouts.

Lynde Shores Conservation Area SUE LEBRECHT

Lynde Shores Conservation Area SUE LEBRECHT

Elsewhere, a 150-metre-long boardwalk extends through waves of head-high bulrushes to an open view of Lynde Creek. A pedestrian road leads south among fields of shrubs to a viewing platform over Cranberry Marsh, where trees make a striking silhouette against Lake Ontario. The road leads onward to a sandy cove on Lake Ontario, strewn with weathered logs.

Two other viewing platforms can be accessed on short paths from Halls Road, just west of the park entrance.

GUIDE NOTES

Location
In Whitby, from Hwy 401, exit Brock St (also Hwy 12; not to be confused with Brock Rd in Ajax), go south to Victoria St (the first set of lights), turn right and go 2.7 km.

Open
Daily, dawn to dusk.

Cost
Parking is 50¢ per half hour to a $2 maximum; $2 coins accepted.

Facilities
None.

Tips
Bring a lawn chair, binoculars, peanuts, unsalted sunflower seeds, and a bird identification book. Wear warm boots. It's best to visit on a calm day after a snowfall, when other food sources are hidden.

Tourism Info
Tourism Durham, 800-413-0017 or 905-723-0023, durecdev@region.durham.on.ca, www.region.durham.on.ca.

More Info
Central Lake Ontario Conservation Authority, 905-579-0411.

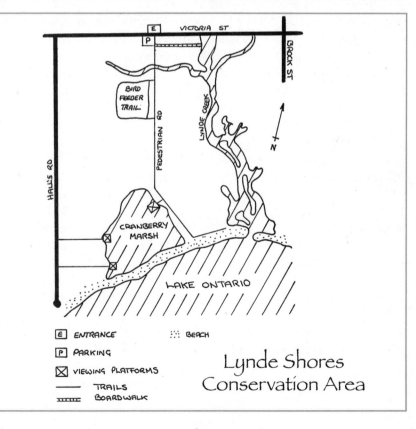

Lynde Shores
Conservation Area

E ENTRANCE
P PARKING
⊠ VIEWING PLATFORMS
—— TRAILS
▥▥▥ BOARDWALK
∴ BEACH

5 *FESTIVAL OF LIGHTS,* CULLEN GARDENS AND MINIATURE VILLAGE
North of Whitby

❋ wander through a miniature village
❋ see massive light displays
❋ visit Santa
❋ watch live entertainment
❋ sing Christmas carols

When: Mid-Nov to the first week of Jan
Highlights: Evenings, when 100,000 miniature lights turn on
Impression: Magical animation

Little Things Count

Little people wearing tiny hats and mittens walk teeny dogs down mini-sidewalks, past thigh-high retail stores decked for Christmas with itsy-bitsy ornaments. In the wee window of an appliance store, a 2-inch TV shows current news. A Santa Claus parade with 40 pint-sized floats drums down Main Street, while a toy train chugs through cottage country.

Cullen Gardens has 160 miniature buildings, set in dwarf landscapes with animation. The models, built to 1/12 scale, are precise replicas of real buildings in Southern Ontario. From the small-town churches, restaurants and shops follow a miniature Highway 400 north past country homes and barns to the resorts on Lake Muskoka, and you're bound to spot a place you'll recognize.

Then go down a hill, into a valley and across a bridge over Lynde Creek, following a path past summer bird-cages filled with seasonal themes: Hockey Night in Canada, gifts around a tree, the story of Scrooge, and others. Enter biblical times with life-sized depictions of Mary and Joseph, no room at the inn, the Star of David, the Wise Men, and Jesus in a manger.

When the sun sets, more than 100,000 miniature lights adorn trees and buildings. Mini streetlamps and car headlights turn on. Huge light sculptures come to life, including a 100-foot-long locomotive, a 75-foot-long sleigh, and Bambi and Thumper chasing each other. Giant Christmas cards, enhanced with fibre-optic lighting, speak their inscriptions. A live Santa sits in his cabin, listening to children's wishes, and live entertainment and Christmas carol sing-alongs are staged in the Tea Room.

GUIDE NOTES

Location
From Hwy 401, go north on Hwy 12 (Brock St) through Whitby, turn left on Taunton Rd and go west 1 km.

Open
Festival of Lights, mid-Nov to early Jan, 10 am to 10 pm. Lights come on at 4 pm. Closed Christmas Day.

Cost
$12 adults, $9 seniors and students, $5 children, ages 2 and under free.

Facilities
Full-service restaurant, snack bar, solarium café, two gift shops.

Events
Kids' Night, Fri with children's performers, wagon rides. Nightly family entertainment Sat to Thurs. New Year's Eve party with dinner, dancing and midnight fireworks; reservations required.

Tourism Info
Tourism Durham, 800-413-0017 or 905-723-0023, durecdev@region.durham.on.ca, www.region.durham.on.ca.

More Info
Cullen Gardens and Miniature Village, 905-686-1600 (in Toronto) or 905-668-6606 or 800-461-1821 (outside of Toronto), cgardens@durham.net, www.cullengardens.com.

6 *SUGARBUSH MAPLE SYRUP FESTIVAL,* BRUCE'S MILL CONSERVATION AREA
Stouffville

❋ hike through sugar bush
❋ participate in pioneer-style maple syrup demonstrations
❋ eat all-day pancake breakfasts
❋ ride horse-drawn wagons

When: First weekend in March to mid-April, daily, with special programming on weekends and during March Break
Highlights: Interactive events and displays, live fiddle music, maple sugar products
Impression: A sweet educational family fiesta

Tree Delicacy
Maple syrup: the watery sap straight from sugar maple trees, evaporated to a thick fluid; a clear fluid with 3-percent sugar content that's boiled to a sugar concentration of 66 percent—40 buckets of sap condensed to one. No additives, no preservatives. Sweet and delicious.

The running of sap through a tree is a spring phenomenon. It starts when there's a combination of cold nights in the low freezing range and warm, sunny days above 4 degrees Celsius. That's when the ground begins to thaw and the roots of trees begin to absorb moisture from the soil.

A pumping action begins. A surge of sap—an essential sugar and mineral nutrient produced by the leaves during summer and stored in the roots over winter—awakens the tree from its dormant winter state, and we tap into it. A hole is drilled into the trunk, about 8 centimetres deep, and a plastic mini-funnel called a spile is inserted, allowing collection of the sap which drips and drools out.

At Bruce's Mill Conservation Area, lines of tubing run everywhere. Spiles in the trees are connected to drop lines, which are connected to thin hoses called lateral lines, which connect to the main line. The main line is hooked to a vacuum pump that draws sap into holding tanks within the sugar shack. The park has a mature sugar bush of about 900 trees—60 to 90 years old on average—which are tapped by some 1,100 spiles, providing for production of upwards of 150 gallons of maple syrup each year.

Sappy Education

Follow the Sugar Maple Trail to various displays to learn all about nature's tasty treat. Historical exhibits tell how native Canadians hollowed a branch for a spile, put an axe split in a tree, collected sap in birch bark buckets, and thickened the sweet water in a hollowed log, using hot rocks from a fire. Displays show how pioneers first used wooden buckets, then ones made of steel with handles that farmers would carry out of the forest on a wooden shoulder-yoke.

On weekends and during March Break, hop on the horse-drawn wagon for a ride into the sugar bush, where interpreters will have you tapping trees and carrying buckets to the huge iron kettles that steam over an open fire. Roll up your sleeves to stir and ladle the sap, and use a back saw to cut logs.

At the sugar shack you can see the mill's modern-day storage tank and vacuum pump, and the wood-fired evaporator, which does its stuff in about four hours. In the canning room, maple syrup is on tap and for sale. At the Pancake House, all-day pancake breakfasts are served, and in the outdoor courtyard, live fiddle music is played at a bonfire.

GUIDE NOTES

Location
From Hwy 404 north of Toronto, go east on Stouffville Rd for 3 km.

Open
In winter, Bruce's Mill Conservation Area is open only during the festival.

Cost
$5 adults, $3 students and seniors, under 4 free.

Facilities
Heated Pancake House, washrooms, Maple Syrup Store.

Tips
The park no longer has trackset cross-country ski trails.

Tourism Info
Tourism Toronto, 800-363-1990 or 416-203-2600, www.tourism-toronto.com.

More Info
Toronto and Region Conservation Authority, 416-661-6600, www.trca.on.ca.

7   ALBION HILLS CONSERVATION AREA
North of Bolton

❄ cross-country ski
❄ skate-ski
❄ toboggan
❄ skate

Highlight: Hilly cross-country skiing with vistas
Impression: Close to Toronto, a convenient, hence popular, recreational outlet for impulsive types

Spontaneously Yours
Situated in the Caledon Hills around the Humber River watershed, Albion Hills offers 26 kilometres of cross-country ski trails. A 10-storey-high toboggan hill lies conveniently off the main access road, and a skating rink stands adjacent to a heated chalet, providing snacks and ski rental equipment.

Trails run up and down through a mix of coniferous and deciduous forest, alongside frozen ponds, marshes and beaver bogs, through meadows and across bridges spanning creeks. Well-marked, mapped, colour-coded and one-way, they are double trackset, with the exception of the Black Trail, which is single trackset and also groomed for skate-skiing. Ten kilometres in length, the Black Trail is the longest and hilliest, with the best lookouts. The Red Trail is another good workout, while kids and beginners have three easier loops to choose from—before they skate laps on the rink and scream on their sleds.

GUIDE NOTES

Location
From Hwy 427 out of Toronto, take Hwy 7 west, then Peel Regional Rd 50 (formerly Hwy 50) through Bolton and continue 8 km north.

Open
Daily, 9 am to 5 pm.

Cost
Admission $4 per person. Cross-country ski trail passes (which include admission) for a full day/half day are $10/$8 adults, $5/$3 for ages 5 to 14, under 5 free, $8/$6 seniors, or $25 for a family pass.

Facilities
Heated chalet with washrooms,
snack bar, open only when skiing
is available.

Rentals
Cross-country ski equipment, $13
adults, $10 children.

Tourism Info
Tourism Toronto, 800-363-1990
or 416-203-2600,
www.tourism-toronto.com.

More Info
Albion Hills Conservation Area,
905-880-4855 or 800-838-9921,
albionhills@trca.on.ca,
Toronto and Region Conservation
Authority,
416-661-6600 ext 203,
www.trca.on.ca.

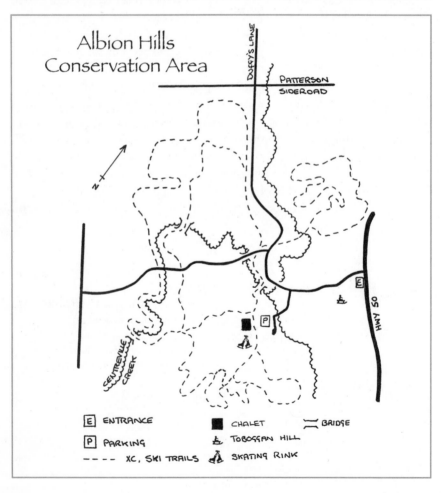

BARRIE/MANSFIELD/COLLINGWOOD

8   MANSFIELD OUTDOOR CENTRE
Mansfield

❉   cross-country ski
❉   skate-ski

Highlights: 40 km network of trackset trails, including a separate 10-km skate-skiing loop in hilly, scenic terrain
Impression: A place traditionalists will appreciate

Peaceful Tracks
The majority of Mansfield's trails lie on top of a moraine—a height of land formed by the debris of a receding glacier. One trail runs along an escarpment edge, providing intermittent views of the Pine River Valley below. Other trails roll deep into the woods, undulating through airy hardwoods and dense, fragrant pine plantations.

Adjacent to the Dufferin County Forest, the centre is based in one of the province's largest contiguous forests south of Barrie and west of Highway 400. A portion of the south slope features an oak forest that has gained designation as an Area of Natural and Scientific Interest. Bambi's hoofprints cross the trails throughout, and large deer bedding areas of leaf piles—some as large as a building—are seen.

The lodge is located at the base of the moraine, so skiers are faced with a long, initial climb. For beginners, however, there are two flat trails that stretch through the flood plain. Snow-making ensures coverage around the base.

Before heading out, warm up with homemade chicken noodle soup, and after, indulge your sweet tooth with a chocolate frosted brownie.

GUIDE NOTES

Location
From Hwy 400, take Hwy 89 west past Alliston and Rosemont, and turn north on Dufferin Rd 18 (Airport Rd) and continue 10 km.

Open
Daily, ski conditions permitting, 9 am to 5 pm.

Cost
Trail fees are $12 adults, $7 children.

Facilities
Cafeteria. Rustic rental cabins for groups of 20 or more; $87 per person, includes two nights lodging, meals and trail passes. Trailer park.

Rentals
Up-to-date cross-country ski equipment, $17 adults, $10 children.

Events/Programs
Ski lessons $10; pre-book.

Tips
If weather conditions on Hwy 400 are nasty, take the quieter route north on Hwy 50.

Tourism Info
Headwaters Country Tourism Association, 800-332-9744 or 519-941-1940.

More Info
Mansfield Outdoor Centre, 705-435-4479, mansfield@sympatico.ca, www.mansfield-outdoors.com.

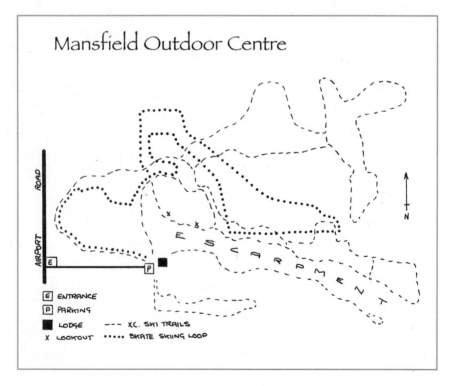

Mansfield Outdoor Centre

E ENTRANCE
P PARKING
■ LODGE   --- X.C. SKI TRAILS
X LOOKOUT   ••••• SKATE SKIING LOOP

9   SNOW VALLEY
West of Barrie

❄ alpine ski and snowboard
❄ ski board
❄ tube

Highlights: Ontario's fastest tubing hill, children's learning area, beginner programs
Impression: A family-oriented facility and a good place for alpine initiation

Family Funland
Snow Valley's Kidz Village is impressive. A segregated area for ages 3 to 5, it features a Magic Carpet Ride (a conveyor-belt-like lift), a wooden fort and a little playground with swings, ropes and tires. The Beginner Adventure Centre, another segregated area, which also has a "magic carpet" plus two handle tows, is a triangular-shaped gentle slope for all ages.

SNOW VALLEY

The resort caters exceedingly well to children—moreover, to all aspiring skiers and snowboarders. Programs galore include bumps, gates, snowboard halfpipe freestyle clinics and an eight-week sampler that runs the gamut. Overall, the hill has an 85-metre vertical drop and 18 trails, almost all of which are lit at night. A handle tow services the halfpipe, and elsewhere a triple, quad, T-bar and belt-loading six-seater—with a low chair height, easy for kids—provide uplift.

New to downhill? Rent ski boards. Ideal for beginners, these mini-skis are short and ridged, with upturned tails and tips, and are ridden without using poles. Only 80 to 100 centimetres long, they are light and easy to manoeuvre. By the afternoon of your first day, you'll likely be tackling intermediate slopes. Commonly referred to as Snowblades—the most prominent brand of its kind—ski boards also offer more versatility and agility than conventional skis, with no less control. Advanced riders carve on edge, go backwards, do spins, jumps and tricks in the halfpipe.

Flying Speed

Tubing is careening down a chute in a rubber inner-tube—no experience required. Snow Valley has eight chutes with a 10-storey plunge that delivers speeds of up to 80 kph! Lit at night, with music echoing over the slopes, the tubing park is serviced by three lifts and has a base chalet for warming up and winding down.

Buddy up with a friend, facing each other, your legs between theirs, front person riding backwards. The more the weight, the faster you go. Ride in a foursome, everyone facing inwards, legs over legs, under arms and on laps. Or hitch up in a raft of six people, three to each side.

The approximately 30-second, gravity-fuelled rush, careening, possibly spinning, will have wind howling in your ears and snow spraying in your face. The tubes are big and bouncy, with nylon bottom covers and two handles, and the chutes have high embankments to keep riders in line. Long level bottoms, uphill ramps and a sprinkling of hay bring you to a halt.

GUIDE NOTES

Location
From Hwy 400 in Barrie, Exit 98 and take Bayfield St (Hwy 26/27) north 5 km to Snow Valley Rd, then go west 6 km.

Open
Daily. Alpine open at 9 am, Mon to 4:30 pm (except holidays to 10 pm), Tues to Sat to 10 pm, Sun to 8 pm. Night skiing starts at 4 pm. Tubing open at 10 am, Mon to 4 pm, Tues to Thurs to 9 pm, Fri and Sat to 11 pm, Sun to 8 pm.

Cost
Alpine start-anytime tickets; choose two-, four-, six-hour or all-day-and-night tickets, ranging from $19 to $35 for adults, less for ages 15 and under. Tubing, one ride is $2, six rides $10, two hours $10, four hours $18, dusk special Tues to Fri $10.

Facilities
Ski chalet with bar and cafeteria, separate tubing chalet.

Rentals
Ski equipment $20, snowboard equipment $30, ski boards rent for $6 per hr.

Events/Programs
Lessons, camps, clinics, various family events.

Tips
Lift and lodging packages to Snow Valley in conjunction with area hotels, inns and bed and breakfasts available through Destination Barrie.

Tourism Info
Destination Barrie, 800-668-9100 or 705-739-9444, fax 705-739-1616, info@barrietourism.on.ca, www.barrietourism.on.ca.

More Info
Snow Valley, 366-7669 (Toronto) or 705-721-7669, www.snowvalley.on.ca.

10 SPRINGWATER PROVINCIAL PARK
Northwest of Barrie

❋ see animals in outdoor enclosures
❋ pull kids on sleighs along pathways
❋ cross-country ski
❋ snowshoe
❋ hike

Highlights: Wandering among animals; skiing easy, uncrowded trails
Impression: A peaceful park for families

Animals Abound
In the heart of Springwater Provincial Park, in outdoor enclosures, are rescued animals that were abused, injured or orphaned. Included are an arctic wolf that was used as a guard dog, an orphaned black bear, and coyotes that were intended for the training of hunting dogs.

Not all of the two dozen animals have known histories. A few of the owls are more than 20 years old. Many of the other birds, including ring-necked pheasants, wild turkeys and mute swans, are offspring of species already captive here before the park's inception in 1958.

The grounds were originally a Victorian-style garden and zoo—the result of a make-work project in the recovering Depression era. The huge pavilion near the park office dates back to 1927. The many ponds were hand-dug.

In one fenced-off pond, a pair of trumpeter swans honk loudly; they are part of the University of Guelph's Trumpeter Swan Breeding Program. White-tailed deer roam a large wooded enclosure, and four beavers are housed in a compound with a concrete lodge and a natural spring-fed pool.

Elsewhere, the park offers 13 kilometres of trackset cross-country ski trails through relatively flat forest that includes 80-year-old stands of red and white pine. For snowshoeing there's a 1.5-kilometre loop, and for hiking, the park road, which forms an approximately 3-kilometre-long loop, makes for an ideal afternoon jaunt.

GUIDE NOTES

Location
From Hwy 400 in Barrie, exit Bayfield St (Hwy 26/27), go north to Midhurst, turn left on Hwy 26 and go 2 km.

Open
Daily, 8 am to 4:30 pm.

Cost
$7.50 per vehicle or $2 per hr, payable at gate box.

Facilities
Heated washroom, plowed parking lot, trail maps in a box by the gate.

Rentals
None.

Tips
Bring correct change for admission fee.

Tourism Info
Destination Barrie,
800-668-9100
or 705-739-9444,
fax 705-739-1616,
info@barrietourism.on.ca,
www.barrietourism.on.ca.

More Info
Springwater Provincial Park,
705-728-7393.

SUE LEBRECHT

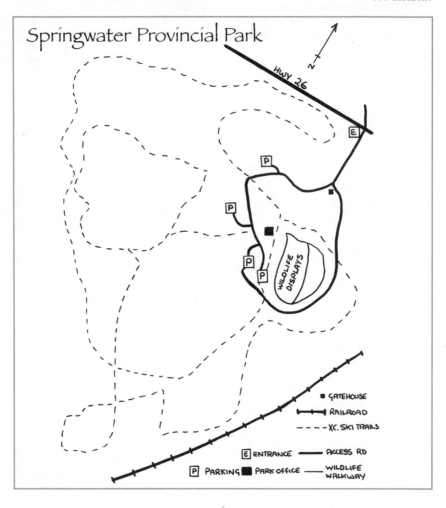

Springwater Provincial Park

HWY 26

N

WILDLIFE DISPLAYS

- ■ GATEHOUSE
- ├┼┤ RAILROAD
- - - XC. SKI TRAILS
- E ENTRANCE ── ACCESS RD
- P PARKING ■ PARK OFFICE ── WILDLIFE WALKWAY

11   HARDWOOD HILLS CROSS-COUNTRY SKI CENTRE
Northeast of Barrie

❊ cross-country ski
❊ skate-ski
❊ backcountry ski
❊ snowshoe
❊ dog walk

EVENTS
➤ Ski with Santa: Dec
➤ Jackrabbit Festival: Feb
➤ Cancer Society Ski-a-thon: March
➤ Spring Fling: March

Highlights: 36 km of cross-country ski trails, snow-making providing reliable conditions
Impression: Southern Ontario's cross-country ski mecca

Initiation, Acceleration
Host to 1,200 skiers on a good day, Southern Ontario's top-notch cross-country ski centre—with a reputation as one of North America's premier facilities—attracts serious, high-performance athletes to skate on skis, rack

HARDWOOD HILLS CROSS-COUNTRY SKI CENTRE

up hard distance and pour sweat. Yet as much as the centre engages the elite, it caters equally well to intermediates and beginners.

Its dense assembly of 36 kilometres of trails is divided into three networks. For first-timers, kids, seniors, and for sledding infants in pulks there's the flat, gentle Meadowlands, with 7.5 kilometres of trails. For intermediates, the Recreational area offers some thrilling hills: Huey, Dewy and Louie, the Rapids, and the Grind. For experts, the Olympic system offers an aggressive, unrelenting challenge.

All trails are wide, well marked, unidirectional, and groomed for both skating and classical techniques, with smooth lanes adjacent to double track-set grooves. Hardwood also has a 6-kilometre ungroomed Wilderness Trail that's open for backcountry skiing, snowshoeing and dog walking. The centre rents modern aluminum snowshoes, with bindings that secure Salomon Profil cross-country ski boots.

GUIDE NOTES

Location
From Hwy 400 in Barrie, continue on the Hwy 400 extension, Exit 111 (Forbes Rd), and go east 10 km.

Open
Daily, weekdays 9 am to 5 pm, weekends 8 am to 5 pm.

Cost
Weekend/weekday trail passes respectively are $15/12.50 adults, $8/$8 for children 8 to12. Ages 7 and under are free.

Facilities
Pro and repair shop, cafeteria, babysitting on weekends. Lodging in a five-bedroom, on-site, bed and breakfast inn, 888-466-2844.

Rentals
Up-to-date cross-country ski equip-ment, $18 adults, $9 for ages 7 and under. Snowshoes, $18 adults (kids' sizes not available).

Programs
Lessons, camps and Jackrabbit Program for kids.

Tips
The cafeteria's freshly baked chocolate chip cookies are not to be missed.

Tourism Info
Destination Barrie,
800-668-9100
or 705-739-9444,
fax 705-739-1616,
info@barrietourism.on.ca,
www.barrietourism.on.ca.

More Info
Hardwood Hills Cross-Country Ski Centre,
800-387-3775 or 705-487-3775,
www.hardwoodhills.on.ca.

12   HORSESHOE RESORT
Northeast of Barrie

* ❄ alpine ski and snowboard
* ❄ cross-country ski
* ❄ skate-ski
* ❄ learn all of the above
* ❄ snowshoe

EVENTS
* ✎ Lantern-lit cross-country ski trails on Sat closest to the full moon
* ✎ Numerous alpine and snowboarding events

Highlights: Alpine bumps and ravines, halfpipes for snowboarders, extensive trails for cross-country skiing
Impression: A busy family hub

Dual Popularity

Attendants are in the parking lot. Tunes waft over the hill base. Cross-country ski and snowshoe trails meander through quiet forest. The Go West Pub gets loud by day's end, and the slopes are lit at night. From the access road, turn left for cross-country skiing or snowshoeing, right for alpine skiing or snowboarding.

For downhill enthusiasts, the resort generally manages to be the first open and the last closed in Southern Ontario, thanks to its aggressive snow-making system. Catering well to snowboarders, it has a halfpipe plus a fun park, and is host to various surf events.

The horseshoe-shaped hill, a 115-metre vertical drop, is laced with 22 trails spaced among trees, including ravine runs and gullies. A high-speed quad chair is one of seven lifts providing uphill service, and night skiing is offered on 14 trails.

For cross-country skiers, trails radiate north, west and south—each direction a different setting. North leads through rolling hills in hardwood forest. West roams flat terrain through an old logging reserve with rows of white oak and pine. South, which includes a groomed lane for skate-skiing, streaks through the golf course, then steadily up to the backside of the alpine hill to a plateau of forest and farmland. The farther you ski, the more challenging the terrain, and the better the views.

The 35-kilometre network is mostly double trackset. Fifty percent of the trails are intermediate level, twenty percent are beginner and the remainder are expert. The trails are presented in a stacked-loop format, so skiers can shorten or extend their trip on impulse. Be sure to experience special full moon night skiing on lantern-lit trails on Saturdays closest to the full moon.

For snowshoeing, the resort offers rentals of modern lightweight models, and has 7 kilometres of marked loops, along with hundreds of unmarked trails in the Copeland Forest and beyond in the Ganaraska Trail System.

GUIDE NOTES

Location
From Hwy 400 in Barrie, continue on the Hwy 400 extension to Exit 117 and go east on Horseshoe Valley Rd for 6 km.

Open
Alpine, mid-Nov to early April, weather permitting, 8:30 am to 4:30 pm, with daily night skiing 4:30 to 10 pm. Cross-country, 8:30 am to 4:30 pm.

Cost
Lift tickets $33 adults full-day, nights $19, lower rates for students, children and seniors, ages under 5 free. Specials include Wed for $17 and Sun nights for $14. Cross-country trail passes full day/half day $14/$10 adults, lower rates for students, children and seniors, ages 6 and under free. Snowshoe trail use is free.

Facilities
Cafeteria, dining room, pro shop, lodging in condos and at the Inn at Horseshoe, which offers skating, indoor swimming, fine dining and a piano bar.

Rentals
Alpine equipment $21, snowboard equipment $27 (credit card deposit required), cross-country equipment $19, snowshoes $19 per day, $13 per half day.

Events/Programs
Lessons, camps, numerous special events for all sport disciplines.

Tips
Bring a lock to secure skis and snowboards, as the resort experiences at least one theft a day—mainly of snowboards. PMCL offers daily bus service to Horseshoe, 416-777-9510.

Tourism Info
Destination Barrie, 800-668-9100 or 705-739-9444, fax 705-739-1616, info@barrietourism.on.ca, www.barrietourism.on.ca.

More Info
Horseshoe Resort, 416-283-2988 in Toronto or 705-835-2790, www.horseshoeresort.com.

13   HIGHLANDS NORDIC
South of Collingwood

* cross-country ski
* skate-ski
* pull kids on trails in pulks
* toboggan

Highlight: 16 km of trackset cross-country ski trails on the Niagara Escarpment

Impression: Good quality, intermediate-level course, with gentle trails for beginners

High Tracks, Far Views
On trails that climb to the top of the Niagara Escarpment, near the highest point of land in Southern Ontario, skiers are granted grand vistas of Georgian Bay, Wasaga Beach, Collingwood and even Barrie on a clear day.

At Highlands Nordic, trails undulate between 420 and 540 metres above sea level. Its 16-kilometre network, groomed wide for both classical and skate-skiing techniques, roams through hardwood forest, across open fields and past limestone outcroppings. The stacked loop system allows skiers flexibility in the length of their trips.

The centre also has a groomed toboggan hill and toboggan rentals.

HIGHLANDS NORDIC

GUIDE NOTES

Location
From Hwy 400 in Barrie take Hwy 26 west to Stayner, continuing straight on Hwy 91. About 3 km past Duntroon, turn left at the first concession and drive 1 km.

Open
Daily, 9 am to 4:30 pm, as snow conditions permit. Closed Christmas Day.

Cost
Weekend/weekday trail passes are $12/$8 adults, $8/$7 juniors and seniors, children under 7 free. Half-day rates available. Tobogganing is $2, but free for pass holders.

Facilities
A renovated barn serves as a ski chalet with a snack bar, pro shop, waxing area and kids' playroom. A big old farmhouse full of amenities offers group accommodation for up to 16 guests.

Rentals
Up-to-date ski rentals, $20 adults, $15 juniors and seniors. Pulks (for pulling children) $10 for half day. Toboggans $1.

Events/Programs
Lessons, kids' classes. Resort partic- ipates in Ski Fest, a North American-wide event held in Jan featuring special introductory pack- ages for first-timers.

Tourism Info
Georgian Triangle Tourist
Association,
705-445-7722,
geotri@georgian.net,
www.georgiantriangle.org.

More Info
Highlands Nordic,
800-263-5017 or 705-444-5017.

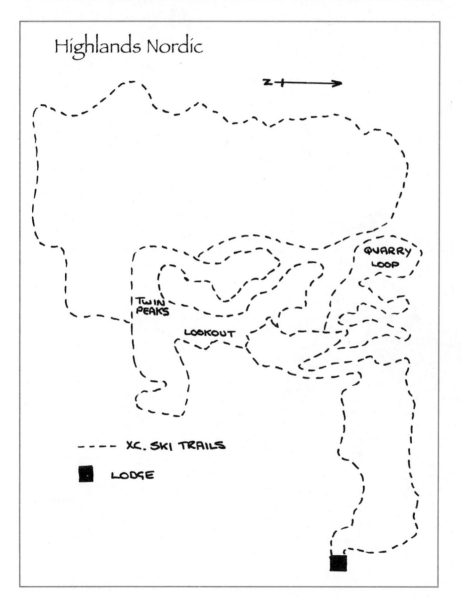

Highlands Nordic

N

QUARRY LOOP

TWIN PEAKS

LOOKOUT

- - - - XC. SKI TRAILS

◼ LODGE

14   BLUE MOUNTAIN
The town of Blue Mountain

❄   alpine ski and snowboard
❄   learn to ski and snowboard
❄   tube

Highlight: Ontario's largest alpine resort
Impression: Hip, happening and fulfilling, by day and aprés

Going Up
To skiers and snowboarders, Blue Mountain requires little introduction. Except to say—if you haven't already heard—that the resort is going to get a facelift.

In January 1999, Intrawest Corp., the owner of Whistler-Blackcomb in B.C. and Tremblant in Quebec, purchased a 50-percent interest in Ontario's largest resort, as well as 100 percent of the land that can be developed at its base.

Preliminary plans include the development of a pedestrian village with restaurants, nightclubs and shops, along with approximately 1,000 condo-hotel units and 200 town homes for sale or rent. In addition, expanded snow-making, the opening of the Orchard, an undeveloped area to the far south, and equipment upgrades are planned.

The first condos are slated to be built in the year 2000, between the central base lodge and the Monterra Pavilion at the central part of Blue's base.

Green at Blue
The resort, which encompasses a 4-kilometre-long stretch of the Niagara Escarpment near Collingwood, has a vertical drop of 216 metres and 15 lifts, including 3 high-speed chairs. Among its trails are four terrain parks with protrusions, undulations and flag-marked jumps, two halfpipes, and a variety of bump runs, including the permanent, machine-maintained Super Mogul Field on Apple Bowl. The Glades, the only treed chute in Ontario, presents a wicked challenge.

Overall, the north end is steep, with diamond runs, and its middle and south slopes are intermediate terrain. Beginners have five separate learning areas, including a full top-to-bottom trail, the Big Baby, at the southern extremity.

The Snow Tubing Park at the south end features five chutes, delivering speeds of up to 60 kph. Check it out—single runs are available for $2. Children must be a minimum height of 42 inches to ride the tubes.

GUIDE NOTES

Location
From Hwy 400 in Barrie, take Hwy 27 north to Hwy 26 west to Stayner. Turn north, still on Hwy 26, to Collingwood, and continue to Blue Mountain Rd.

Open
Alpine, Dec 1 to Mar 31, snow permitting, 9 am to 4:30 pm, with daily night-skiing Christmas Break to March Break, 4:30 to 10 pm. Tubing, open days and nights, times vary.

Cost
Lift tickets are adults $40 per day, $45 per day and night, lower rates for children and seniors, under 5 free. Tubing, $2 single ride, $12 for 8 rides, $15 for 12 rides.

Facilities
Three fully serviced base lodges.

Rentals
Available at South and Central Base Lodges. Ski equipment $24, snowboard equipment $34.

Events/Programs
Lessons, camps, numerous special events, beginner lift, lesson and rental packages. The resort also participates in National Ski and Snowboard Week, held annually the third week in Jan, featuring discount first-timer ski and snowboard packages.

Tips
For après skiing, head first to Joz's at the Blue Mountain Inn.

Tourism Info
Georgian Triangle Tourist Association, 705-445-7722, geotri@georgian.net, www.georgiantriangle.org.

More Info
Blue Mountain, 24-hour service, including accommodation reservations, 416-869-3799 in Toronto or 705-445-0231, www.bluemountain.ca.

SPORTOGRAPHY,
BLUE MOUNTAIN
RESORT

BRONTE CREEK PROVINCIAL PARK

BURLINGTON/MILTON

15 BRONTE CREEK PROVINCIAL PARK
West of Oakville

* ❄ cross-country ski
* ❄ skate
* ❄ toboggan
* ❄ tour a century farmhouse
* ❄ let kids loose in a play barn

EVENTS
* Community Christmas Festival: First Sun in Dec to first Sun in Jan
* Maple Syrup Festival: Weekends in March and daily during March Break
* Murder Mystery Dinner: During the Community Christmas Festival

Highlights: Decorated Christmas trees, cross-country skiing alongside a deep ravine, tobogganing, showing farm animals to children
Impression: Family winter wonderland with activities galore

Pockets of Play
Kids tear across bridges, climb tires and slides as they run, screaming, throughout a two-storey Play Barn. They tow parents through stables housing goats, sheep, cows, pigs, rabbits and donkeys. They toboggan down a man-made hill, skate laps around a rink, and try to figure out the logistics of cross-country skiing in trackset trails.

And while the recreational oasis of Bronte Creek Provincial Park is mainly geared to families, adults without children are also welcome to come and play. The high toboggan hill is a thrill at any age. The artificially cooled skating rink, which is lit at night and flooded with music, is a romantic site. Cross-country ski trails—20 kilometres worth—lead past 100-year-old trees, through open fields, and along the edge of a deep-cut ravine with Twelve Mile Creek running through it. Blue jays and chickadees flit through the forest, deer and rabbit tracks cross the trail, and hawks are often seen overhead.

At the south end, you can tour a furnished Victorian farmhouse. Built in 1899, staffed by costumed interpreters, and decorated with period Christmas ornaments throughout December, the Spruce Lane Farm House offers insight into home life at the turn of the century. A fully operational farm museum, it also has adjacent barns—restored on original foundations—with cattle, horses, pigs and fowl.

Trees and Sap

Community Christmas, a four-week-long festival and fundraiser for the Children's Wish Foundation, features company-decorated trees in the tent-like structure of the Recreation Complex. Wooden fences lit with lights line the laneway, and Santa ho-ho-hos inside. Various local choirs and bands perform carols, a barbecue sizzles, visitors vote for their favourite trees, kids make crafts, and horse-drawn sleighs take groups on 45-minute-long rides.

The Maple Syrup Festival includes a pancake tent, a candy shanty, horse-drawn wagon rides and a Syrup Trail, showing how sap was collected and maple syrup produced over the last 300 years.

GUIDE NOTES

Location
Between Oakville and Burlington. From the QEW, take Exit 109 and go north on Burloak Dr for 0.5 km.

Open
Daily, 8 am to 9:30 pm. Closed from noon on Dec 24 and on Christmas Day. Spruce Lane Farm House and Nature Centre, weekends only, 10 am to 4 pm. Children's Farm and Play Barn, daily, 9 am to 4 pm. Park Store,

Mon to Fri, 6 to 9 pm, Sat and Sun 10 am to 9 pm. Skating rink, from the first weekend in Dec to March Break, weather permitting.

Cost
$3 adults, $1.75 ages 4 to 17, $2.25 seniors, to a maximum of $12 per vehicle.

Facilities
Heated changing rooms, snack bar, evening-lit skating rink.

Rentals
Cross-country ski equipment $8. Skates $3.

Events/Programs
Community Christmas, 6 to 9 pm weekdays, noon to 8 pm weekends and during Christmas holidays. Murder Mystery Dinner during Community Christmas. Maple Syrup Festival, weekends in March and daily during March Break, 10 am to 4 pm. Group horse-drawn wagon rides.

Tips
Other special events monthly; call for more information.

Tourism Info
Oakville Chamber of Commerce, 905-845-6613.

More Info
Bronte Creek Provincial Park, 905-827-6911, Park Store (offering rentals) ext 221, www.ontarioparks.com.

Bronte Creek Provincial Park

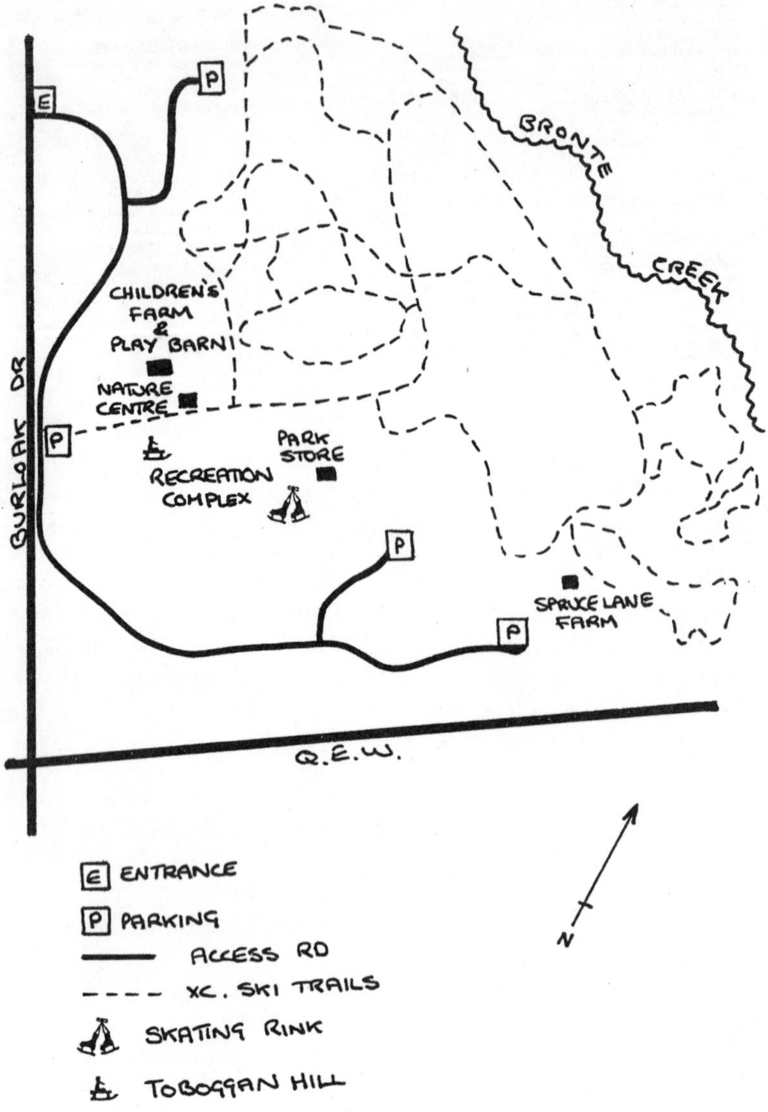

BURLOAK DR

BRONTE CREEK

CHILDREN'S FARM & PLAY BARN

NATURE CENTRE

PARK STORE

RECREATION COMPLEX

SPRUCE LANE FARM

Q.E.W.

N

E ENTRANCE
P PARKING
—— ACCESS RD
- - - - XC. SKI TRAILS
SKATING RINK
TOBOGGAN HILL

16   HILTON FALLS CONSERVATION AREA
West of Milton

* cross-country ski
* cook-out at a fire ring
* see mill ruins and a frozen waterfall
* hand-feed chickadees and nuthatches

EVENT
* Moonlight Skiing: Fri nights closest to the full moon

Highlights: Skiing to a campfire beside an icefall and hand-feeding birds
Impression: An enchanting escape

Romancing the Snow
Pack hot dogs and marshmallows, and pick up a free bag of birdseed from
the Visitors' Centre before skiing out to the 10-metre-high icefall, where a
campfire awaits. Cook your lunch and roast your treats. Sit on a bench, lean
against stone walls and feed the birds. Chickadees and nuthatches, one by
one, will land on your outstretched hand for a seed.

The site of three separate sawmills that operated between 1835 and
1867, Hilton Falls is also said to have been a stop on the underground rail-

HALTON REGION CONSERVATION AUTHORITY

road escape route used by Black slaves fleeing the United States in the 1850s and 1860s.

The on-site fire is started by park staff on weekend mornings, and skiers keep it going all day with the wood stack provided. Another fire ring, stocked with wood but not initially lit by staff, lies at the far end of the Beaver Dam Loop that leads skiers through frozen wetland.

Located on the Niagara Escarpment with two tributaries of Sixteen Mile Creek running through it, the park offers 15.5 km of groomed and trackset trails in diverse topography. The Red Oak Trail runs around a reservoir bordered by a ridge, affording high open views.

Come first thing in the morning and there's a good chance of seeing deer. Preregister for a moonlight event and join a guided ski tour in the cast of a full moon.

GUIDE NOTES

Location
From Hwy 401, take Hwy 25 north to Regional Rd 9 and go west 6 km. From the QEW, take Guelph Line north through Campbellville to Regional Rd 9 and go east for 4 km.

Open
Daily, 8:30 am to 4:30 pm. Closed Christmas Day.

Cost
$3.25 adults, $2.75 seniors, $2.25 ages 5 to 14, ages 4 and under free; includes trail passes.

Facilities
Visitors' Centre with washrooms and snack bar, two ringed firepits for cook-outs.

Rentals
None

Events
Preregistration required for the guided moonlight ski jaunts, weather permitting.

Tips
Bring marshmallows, hot dogs and a camera.

Tourism Info
Milton Chamber of Commerce, 905-878-0581, fax 905-878-4972.

More Info
Hilton Falls Conservation Area, 905-854-0262, fax 905-854-2303. Halton Region Conservation Authority, 905-336-1158, www.hrca.on.ca.

Hilton Falls Conservation Area

HILTON
FALLS

RESERVOIR

---- XC. SKI
        TRAILS

~~~ STREAMS

WETLANDS

FIRE RINGS

P PARKING

VISITOR
CENTRE

N

CAMPBELLVILLE RD
REGIONAL RD 9

17   MOUNTSBERG CONSERVATION AREA
Campbellville

* see birds of prey, buffalo and elk
* enter a barn full of animals
* hike nature trails
* skate on a pond
* cross-country ski
* snowshoe

EVENTS
* Birds of Prey: Live presentations, weekends at 1 and 3 pm
* Owl Prowls: Weekends in late Jan and early Feb
* Maple Syrup Days: Weekends in late Feb to mid-April and daily during March Break

Highlight: Live raptor presentations
Impression: Educational wildlife facility

Enrapturing
The Raptor Centre at Mountsberg is dedicated to helping birds of prey. Its treat-and-release avian hospital receives up to 300 injured birds annually, and raptors with permanent injuries are housed in large cages. Its bird-banding program is Canada's second largest. The exhibit area is full of educational videos and displays, including one on the relocation program at Pearson International Airport, where each year up to 200 birds of prey are caught and released in safer areas.

Live raptor presentations are given on weekends in a large net-covered flyway. A Birds of Prey Trail leads among the caged hawks, owls and eagles, with signs telling where the birds came from, when and why, along with their diet, vocalizations, habitat and population distribution.

Other trails—14 kilometres worth—also beg exploration. Hike the Wildlife Walkway to elk and buffalo compounds. Snowshoe the Nature Trivia Trail to learn tidbits about the environment. Cross-country ski the groomed—but not trackset—6-kilometre Lakeshore Lookout along the edge of a large reservoir on a tributary of Bronte Creek, or the 6.5-kilometre Pioneer Creek through deciduous forest with creek crossings, past lime kilns and pioneer fences. If hiking, please stay off the tracks.

Skate on a frozen pond. The historic barn, with stonework dating from 1872, houses sheep, rabbits and huge Percheron horses.

Delicious Transformation

During Maple Syrup Days, horse-drawn wagons deliver families a short distance into the forest, where shiny silver buckets are hooked on trees under dripping spiles, and where interpreters in various cabins demonstrate maple syrup production.

Walk the half-kilometre-long Sugar Bush Trail, among displays, to learn the history of maple syrup, from its discovery by North American natives to modern production methods. Enter the Sugar House to see how 30 litres of raw sap are boiled down to one litre of golden syrup. Visit the Candy House to sample maple sugar. A Product House offers cookbooks and syrup for sale, while syrup-smothered pancakes and sausages are available in the Picnic Pavilion.

GUIDE NOTES

Location
From Hwy 401, take Guelph Line south 1 km to Campbellville Rd, go west 3 km to Milborough Line, then north 1 km.

Open
Weekends and holidays, 10 am to 4 pm.

Cost
$4 adults, $2.75 ages 5 to 14, under 4 free. Special group rates available.

Facilities
Raptor Centre, Visitors' Centre with washrooms, gift shop, eating area, picnic shelter.

Rentals
Snowshoes available.

Events/Programs
Owl Prowls include a slide show, a live owl presentation, and an evening hike with a naturalist; preregistration required. Evening sleigh rides for groups are available.

Tips
The entrance fee at Mountsberg will also get you into nearby Crawford Lake and into Hilton Falls Conservation Area on the same day.

Tourism Info
Festival Country,
800-267-3399, 519-756-3230,
festival@niagara-midwest-ont.com,
www.niagara-midwest-ont.com.

More Info
Mountsberg Conservation Area
905-854-2276,
mtsberg@hrca.on.ca,
Halton Region Conservation
Authority, 905-336-1158,
www.hrca.on.ca.

Mountsberg Conservation Area

⛺ SKATING RINK

E ENTRANCE

P PARKING

T OBSERVATION TOWER

T

TOWN LINE

N

~ MOUNTSBERG RESERVOIR ~

T

SUGAR BUSH

P

WILDLIFE WALKWAY

E

■ INTERPRETIVE CENTRE & HISTORIC BARN

▲ BIRDS OF PREY CENTRE

+—+ RAILROAD

—— TRAILS

━━ ACCESS ROAD

18   CRAWFORD LAKE CONSERVATION AREA
Campbellville

❋ tour a reconstructed Iroquoian Village
❋ cross-country ski
❋ snowshoe
❋ hike
❋ participate in kids' activities

EVENTS
🍃 Guided Village Tours: Weekends at 1 and 3 pm
🍃 Sweetwater Season: Weekends late Feb to mid-April and daily during March Break
🍃 Snowshoe Adventure: Select days in Jan and Feb

Highlights: Village tours, trekking around a meromictic lake, Escarpment lookouts
Impression: A remarkable piece of archaeological detective work

Cultivating Culture
Surrounded by a palisade of protective wooden poles, the reconstructed 15th-century Iroquoian Village is where approximately 250 people once lived in five longhouses. More than 10,000 artifacts were uncovered at this site by archaeologists during a 15-year-long excavation beginning in 1973.

HALTON REGION CONSERVATION AUTHORITY

Located on the Niagara Escarpment with the Bruce Trail running through it, the park also offers a 12-kilometre network of trails, 8 kilometres of which are sometimes groomed and trackset for cross-country skiing. The hiking highlight is the elevated boardwalk around Crawford Lake. Small and deep, with little oxygen and limited circulation, the lake has preserved in distinct layers the leaves, seeds and pollen that have sunk to its bottom over the past 1,000 years. Studies of the sediment, which revealed corn pollen from cultivated crops, led to the unearthing and accurate dating of the village.

Set on a hill, the village includes burial platforms, firepits, a games field, areas for making pottery and maple syrup, and two bark-covered longhouses full of animal hides, working tools and bundles of braided corn. In the Wolf Clan Longhouse a simulated archaeological dig area has been set up. The adjacent Interpretive Centre features artifacts along with displays, maps and photographs outlining the history of the original village. For youngsters, the centre also offers weekend discovery hunts.

For cross-country skiing, the 2.7-kilometre Woodland Trail leads past the village and lake through gently rolling forest, while the 5.2-kilometre Pine Ridge Trail loops through pine plantations and fields.

GUIDE NOTES

Location
From Hwy 401, take Guelph Line
5 km south to Steeles Ave and turn
east. From the QEW, take Guelph
Line north to Steeles Ave and turn
east.

Open
Weekends and holidays only, 10 am
to 4 pm; daily during March Break.

Cost
$4 adults, $3.25 seniors, $2.75 for
ages 5 to 14, ages 4 and under free.

Facilities
Visitors' Centre with exhibit gallery,
gift shop, refreshments, washrooms.

Rentals
None

Events/Programs
The Snowshoe Adventure offers
guided educational hikes with
special-event snowshoe rentals;
preregister. Sweetwater Season
includes storytelling, hands-on
demonstrations, samples of traditional cornbread dipped in maple
syrup and craft-making workshops.
Organized birthday parties.

Tips
The entrance fee at Crawford Lake
will also get you into nearby Mountsberg and Hilton Falls Conservation
Areas on the same day.

Tourism Info
Festival Country,
800-267-3399, 519-756-3230,
festival@niagara-midwest-ont.com,
www.niagara-midwest-ont.com.

More Info
Crawford Lake Conservation Area,
905-854-0234, Halton Region
Conservation Authority,
905-336-1158, www.hrca.on.ca.

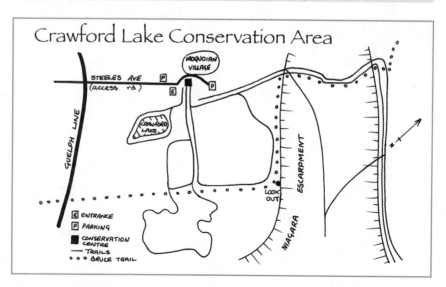

HAMILTON/PARIS/ELMIRA

19   DUNDAS VALLEY CONSERVATION AREA
Ancaster

* hike
* bird-watch
* snowshoe
* toboggan
* dog walk
* cross-country ski

EVENTS
* Night Hike: Mid-Dec
* Animal Tracking: Last weekend in Jan and mid-Feb
* Snowshoe Workshops: Mid-Jan and mid-Feb
* Owl Prowl: First weekend in Feb
* Coyote Howl: Mid-March

Highlights: Tobogganing, long hikes, picture-perfect winter scenes
Impression: Extremely scenic and extensive winter stomping ground

Big Slide, Long Trek
The toboggan hill of your childhood dreams lies near the park's main entrance. A mighty mound 150 metres high, it starts with a steep plunge and continues with a long gentle slope that nevertheless accelerates your speed all the way to the bottom, where it levels out for you to roll off in a fit of laughter. A berm serves as a road barrier.

Past the entrance, into the forest, enter a setting of Christmas-card pictures: snowdrops on evergreens, icefalls on rock cliffs, crystal creeks through white valleys. Trails weave through an incredible variety of settings—along ridges, down ravines, across meadows, past flowing and frozen cascades, historic ruins, plateaus of rock and high points with panoramic views.

Surrounded by the Niagara Escarpment, the huge, hilly, heavily wooded park features a 40-kilometre network of 5 main wide trails and 10 minor narrow trails, plus a 32-kilometre-long rail-trail connecting Hamilton to Brantford. Arrive in the morning and you may be breaking trail; come in the afternoon and follow footsteps.

Main trails are well trodden, minor trails are best for snowshoeing, and the rail-trail—the only level stretch in the park—lets you speed on cross-

73

country skis. The rail-trail isn't trackset, however, and elsewhere in the undulating terrain, only 5 kilometres of trail are trackset, and these tend to be discourteously hiked upon.

The parking lot is packed on bright sunny weekends. Visitors come to hike in the morning, have lunch at the Trail Centre, then hike in the afternoon. Birders spy on cardinals, blue jays, chickadees, and an assortment of woodpeckers, including the pileated, "Woody Woodpecker" type, that flit through the forest. Winter-loving mountain bikers, equestrians and runners also frequent the trails.

Before heading out, purchase the park's topographical Adventure Map from the Trail Centre or pick up one of the free brochures that outline specific trails—or prepare to get lost. Dundas Valley Conservation Area is a collage of properties, laced with trails and partitioned by roads. It's easy to get disoriented.

Howls, Prowls, Tracks and Treks

Annual winter events include a night hike called Echoes of the Past. Lanterns line the walkway to the Trail Centre, where participants are then led to the Hermitage, the remains of a commanding stone mansion. Afterwards, a campfire and hot chocolate await. The Owl Prowl and Coyote Howl, also held in the evening, feature illustrated talks followed by hikes, with naturalists hooting and howling in an effort to evoke real response. Animal Tracking looks at the footprints of wildlife, while Snowshoe Workshops include snowshoe rentals and a guided trek.

GUIDE NOTES

Location
From the QEW, take Hwy 403 to Main St W (a three-lane main artery) and go 2.3 km into the town of Dundas. From the "Welcome to Dundas" sign, go 1.3 km to Governor's Rd (there's a Tim Horton's at the intersection) and turn left. Drive 3 km west and watch for the Dundas Valley Conservation Area Park sign. Continue 0.5 km past the sign then turn left into the park's main entrance. The main parking lot is 0.5 km past the gate, and the Trail Centre is a short walk from the lot.

Alternatively, from the intersection of Hwys 5, 8 and 52, go south on Hwy 52 to Regional Rd 299 (Governor's Rd) at Copetown, turn left (east) at the flashing lights and drive 6 km to the second conservation sign and turn right.

Open
9 am to 5 pm.

Cost
$5 per vehicle, in a coin-operated gate.

Facilities
Trail Centre open weekends and holidays, with trail maps, soup, snacks, hot dogs, hot chocolate, refreshments.

Rentals
None.

Events/Programs
Preregistration is required for all events; contact the Trail Centre. Customized group outings, for 10 to 20 people, and organized school groups can be arranged with Down to Earth, Environmental Education and Leadership Programs, 905-627-3140.

Tips
Bring $5 in loonies and $2 coins to enter. Wear gaiters with your boots.

Splurge $8 for a plastic-coated, topographical Adventure Map. Check the park's website for trail conditions and event dates.

Cautions
Trails get slick with heavy use, and tend to get icy in March.

Tourism Info
Greater Hamilton Tourist Information Centre, 800-263-8590 or 905-546-2666, www.hamilton-went.on.ca, Conservation Lands of Ontario, 888-376-2212, www.conservationlands.com.

More Info
Dundas Valley Conservation Area, 905-627-1233, trail conditions ext 1, or Hamilton Region Conservation Authority, 905-525-2181, www.hamrca.on.ca.

20 VALENS CONSERVATION AREA
North of Flamborough

❄ winter camp
❄ cross-country ski
❄ skate
❄ ice fish

EVENT
🦫 Winter Beach Party: Late Jan or early Feb

Highlights: Winter camping, close but seemingly far away from metropolis
Impression: A quiet, rugged escape with the opportunity to rough it overnight

Suburban Wilderness
With hot showers, heated washrooms, a pavilion with a fireplace, laundry facilities and a general store close by, Valens Conservation Area is an ideal place to try winter camping.

Slip $5 into the gate box, grab a park brochure, drive into the camping area, pick a site among the tall white pines and pitch your tent. Or alternatively, park your trailer. Valens Conservation Area offers year-round camping, including electrical sites, each with a firepit and picnic table. However, you'll likely only be in the company of a half-dozen others. The majority of winter visitors simply come for the day, for a quiet escape.

Bring a shovel and clear a skating rink in the summer swimming area of the reservoir. Drill a hole in the ice to fish for northern pike. Explore the 10 kilometres of groomed and trackset cross-country ski trails that roam through the campground and surrounding forest.

A 4-kilometre loop around the reservoir includes a 300-metre stretch of boardwalk that cuts across a marsh, where stumps and muskrat dens protrude from the flat frozen surface. Trail extensions lead through open fields, mature forest, pine plantations, and to a five-storey-high lookout tower. Hikers and snowshoers are requested to walk to the side of the groomed trails—not on them.

Valens Conservation Area
HAMILTON REGION CONSERVATION AUTHORITY

GUIDE NOTES

Location
From Hwy 401, take Hwy 6 south, turn right on Regional Rd 97 and follow signs. From Hwy 403, take Hwy 6 north, turn left on Regional Rd 97 and follow signs.

Open
Daily, sun-up to sundown.

Cost
$5, payable by coin only, at the gate; $2 coins accepted. Camping fees per night are $19 for non-electrical, $23 for electrical or partially serviced; park staff will register you at your site, deducting the admission from the camping fee.

Facilities
83 winter campsites, 34 of which have electrical hook-up.

Rentals
Ice huts.

Events
The Winter Beach Party is a one-day event with snowshoeing.

Tips
Dee's General Store lies one km west of the park.

Cautions
Hunting is allowed at the park between Sept 25 and Dec 20. During this period, on Mon, Wed and Sat, campers must remain in the

WEST: HAMILTON/PARIS/ELMIRA

campground from 5 am to noon
(unless leaving area by vehicle).

Tourism Info
Greater Hamilton Tourist
Information Centre,
800-263-8590 or 905-546-2666,
www.hamilton-went.on.ca.

More Info
Valens Conservation Area,
905-525-2183 or 519-621-6029,
valens@hamrca.on.ca.

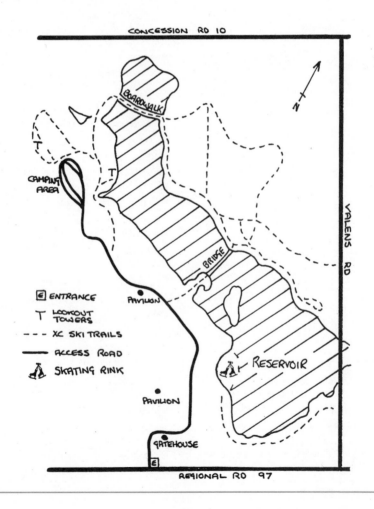

Valens Conservation Area

21   WESTFIELD HERITAGE VILLAGE
Rockton

❄   walk in and among historical buildings
❄   hike to stone ruins
❄   watch costumed interpreters demonstrate old trades
❄   see forgotten Yuletide customs

EVENTS
❧   Christmas in the Country: Weekends in Dec
❧   A Christmas Table: First two Sun in Dec
❧   A Moveable Feast: First three Sat in Dec
❧   Sweet Taste of Spring: Sun in March, plus a few days during
    March Break
❧   Miss Muffin Gets Married: Feb on Sat closest to Valentine's Day

Highlights: Historical buildings, dinner programs
Impression: A fascinating glimpse of life as it was in Southern Ontario in
simpler times

Time Warp
Pass through the gates of time. Westfield Heritage Village features 33
historical buildings dating from the late 1700s to 1917. There are residential homes, a general store, church, school, blacksmith shop, print shop, drug
store, sawmill, smokehouse, carriage barn, train station and others—each
authentic. People once lived, worked, worshipped, socialized and celebrated
in these buildings in Southern Ontario. Many of the buildings were saved
from demolition; some were donations. All were painstakingly moved to this
site and restored to their original form.

   The one-room schoolhouse, built at a time when attendance was not
compulsory, comes from Cathcart, near London. The log chapel, believed
to be the oldest church in Ontario, comes from Brantford, where it was used
on the Six Nations Reserve until 1854. The prominent church, where
women were seated to the right and men on the left until 1870, comes from
Mountsberg.

   A one-kilometre pathway leads through the village-like setting. A tour
map provides information about the buildings. And from the mud-block
house to the Jerseyville Train Station, the evolution of more than 100 years
of our culture unfolds. Moreover, the Woods Trail, behind the railway station, leads through mixed forest and marshland to thick lilac patches, a
Sugar Shack and old stone farm ruins.

Westfield Heritage Village
HAMILTON REGION CONSERVATION AUTHORITY

Self-guided tours of the exteriors can be taken daily, but the village comes alive on Sundays and holidays between March and December, with open buildings staffed by costumed interpreters demonstrating various trades. The village also presents a number of special programs.

Christmas and Culinary Classics

Christmas in the Country shows the Yuletide season through the Georgian, Victorian, Edwardian and World War I eras. Visitors are introduced to long-forgotten customs and can witness the changing tide of celebrations, from those of the early European settlers to modern North American traditions. Horse-drawn wagons offer rides, and the Gift Shop and restaurant are open.

A Christmas Table, for up to 80 guests, is an extensive Yuletide feast featuring a Christmas goose, and stuffing made to Queen Victoria's specifications. The evening is topped with carol singing and storytelling around a bonfire. Reservations required.

The Moveable Feast invites guests to eat their way through history in a roving four-course meal. Led by the ghost of Christmas, participants—a maximum of eight people—begin by breaking bread at a late 1700s farmstead and end at an early 1900s Dry Goods Store for coffee, tea, plum pudding and a surprise. Reservations required.

When Miss Muffin gets married to a soldier in a re-enactment of a wedding in 1812, you're a guest at the reception, feasting on fare of the era, while dancing and singing the evening away. Reservations required.

In the Sweet Taste of Spring, visitors join Canadian settlers as they collect sap, tell legends and produce maple syrup using native, pioneer and modern methods. Horse-drawn wagons offer rides, and pancakes and sausages smothered in maple syrup are served at the Ironwood Teahouse.

GUIDE NOTES

Location
From the QEW, take Hwy 403 to Hwy 6, go north to Hwy 5, go west to Hwy 8, then north to Regional Rd 552, turn right and go 1.5 km.

Open
Daily for self-guided outdoor tours. Closed Dec 21 to 31. Buildings are open only on Sun and holidays, March to Dec, 12:30 to 4 pm.

Cost
$5.50 adults, $4.50 seniors, $2.50 ages 6 to 12, under 6 free. Miss Muffin Gets Married, A Christmas Table, The Moveable Feast, each $42 per person.

Facilities
Wedding functions, gift shop, restaurant.

Tips
Preregister as early as Sept for a seat in either of the Christmas dinner programs.

Tourism Info
Greater Hamilton Tourist Information Centre, 800-263-8590 or 905-546-2666, www.hamilton-went.on.ca, Conservation Lands of Ontario, 888-376-2212, www.conservationlands.com.

More Info
Westfield Heritage Village, 519-621-8851 or 888-319-4722, westfld@worldchat.com, www.hamrca.on.ca.

PINEHURST LAKE CONSERVATION AREA

22   PINEHURST LAKE CONSERVATION AREA
North of Paris

❋   cross-country ski

Highlight: Cross-country skiing among hills, ravines and valleys
Impression: A scenic and varied setting

Ring Around the Lake

Pinehurst Lake, an oval-shaped kettle lake formed in glacial times by melt-ing ice, lies at the heart of the park. Trees line its shore and hills surround it. Summer camping areas have been developed adjacent to it, north and south, and bordering these, in the furthest reaches, are steeper hills with hardwood bush and evergreen plantations. To the northeast, the old "Morton Property" is a mixed agricultural plot that's being reclaimed by nature. It too is hilly and surrounded by forest.

Swooping cross-country ski trails loop through all sections of the park—around the lake, up and down hills and ravines, along ridges, through val-leys, meadows and hollows. Groomed and trackset, they follow wide roadways and narrow hiking trails. The farther you ski, the steeper the ter-rain, the more intimate the setting, and the better your chances of seeing deer and other wildlife.

Host to 300 people on a good Saturday, the park offers 13 kilometres of trails, all mapped, colour coded and unidirectional.

GUIDE NOTES

Location
From Hwy 401, take Hwy 24 south into Cambridge and continue south on Hwy 24A (Regional Rd 75) towards Paris. After passing Waterloo Regional Rd 49, entrance is on your left. Alternatively, from the QEW, take Hwy 403 to Rest Acres Rd north to Paris and follow conservation area signs.

Open
Daily, 9 am to 4 pm, as conditions permit. Closed Christmas Day, Boxing Day and New Year's Day.

Cost
Trail passes $4 adults, $2.25 for ages 6 to 14, ages 5 and under free.

Facilities
Hot snack concession, change area, washrooms.

Rentals
Three-pin binding system skis avail-able, including children's sizes, $8 per person.

83

Tourism Info
Tourism Brantford,
800-265-6299
or 519-751-9900,
tourism@city.brantford.on.ca,
www.city.brantford.on.ca.

More Info
Pinehurst Lake Conservation Area,
519-442-4721,
www.grandriver.on.ca.

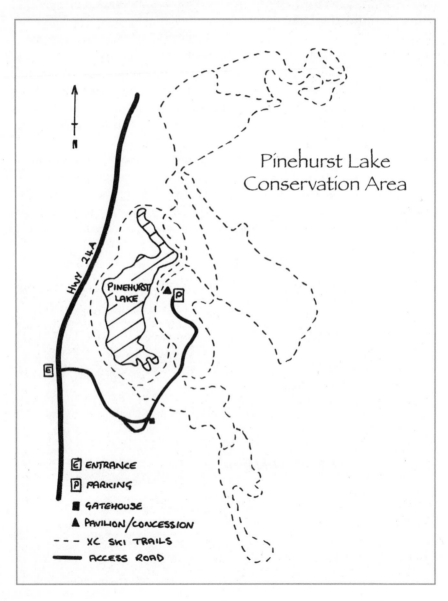

Pinehurst Lake
Conservation Area

HWY 24A

PINEHURST
LAKE

E ENTRANCE
P PARKING
■ GATEHOUSE
▲ PAVILION/CONCESSION
- - - XC SKI TRAILS
▬▬▬ ACCESS ROAD

23 *MAPLE SYRUP FESTIVAL*, ELMIRA
North of Waterloo

When: A one-day event on first Sat in April
Highlights: Mennonite country
Impression: An old-fashioned family affair

Sweet Country Culture

Ontario's largest and oldest Maple Syrup Festival, attracting upwards of 80,000 visitors, is staged in Mennonite country by the little town of Elmira, population 7,300. Year 2000 will mark the 36th annual festival.

The town's main street—closed to traffic for the day—is transformed into a kilometre-long outdoor mall, with 150 vendors selling crafts and food. A pancake tent opens at 7:30 am, and the pancake-flipping contest begins at 10 am. Local churches are used as restaurants, with home-style meals. The Farmers' Shed is host to Old MacDonald's Farm, with a petting zoo and hay maze. There's a quilt show at the high school, an antiques show at the arena, and a toy show at the Carriage Hall.

Visitors park in factory lots on the outskirts of town, where tractor-drawn hay wagons provide shuttle service. From town, school buses run

ELMIRA MAPLE SYRUP FESTIVAL

trips to Mennonite sugar bushes, where sap-to-syrup production is demonstrated. St. Jacob's Country Livery provides horse-drawn trolley tours around the festival. Charter buses offer hour-and-a-half-long Country Heritage Tours, with stops at a buggy factory, a Mennonite dairy farm, and the covered bridge—Ontario's only—in West Montrose.

GUIDE NOTES

Location
From Hwy 401, take Hwy 6 north through Guelph to Hwy 7 west to Regional Rd 86 north to town.

Cost
Parking and festival admission is free, but there are small fees for pancakes and tours. All money raised goes to local charities.

Tips
From Waterloo, a restored 1950s streamliner provides train transportation to the festival. En route, you can get off at St. Jacobs and enjoy the market before carrying on to Elmira, 519-746-1950.

More Info
Elmira Chamber of Commerce, 519-669-2605, www.elmiramaplesyrup.com.

OWEN SOUND/HANOVER

24 HEADQUARTERS CONSERVATION AREA
South of Hanover

❊ snowshoe
❊ hike
❊ cross-country ski
❊ see a sulphur spring that never freezes
❊ feed fish and birds
❊ roam through a wildlife sanctuary

EVENT
❧ Christmas in the Country: second weekend of Dec

Highlights: A sulphur spring, wildlife sanctuary, fish and bird feeding
Impression: A medley of intriguing exploration

Follow Your Nose
No matter how cold it gets, the sulphur spring at Headquarters Conservation Area never freezes. In fact, the colder the temperature the more it steams on its course through frosted white forest.

Don snowshoes—available on-site—and follow the blue-blazed trees to the spring's source—a 3-metre-deep, pungent-smelling hole. The crystal-clear flow that wells from below, which remains at 9 degrees Celsius year-round, supplies water to the park's three ponds. They too never freeze.

The 20-minute-long trail first runs past a Wildlife Sanctuary, with a viewing barn of pheasants and fowl, and a fenced field of deer and swans. It then follows alongside the stream, among snow-laden cedars, dogwoods and other lowland trees, where several bridges let you gaze into the water. Blue and purple mineral formations protrude like stalagmites from the creek bed. Green plant-life waves along the banks.

A total of 4 kilometres of trails loop through the park. For cross-country skiers, a trackset trail leads to hilly forest at its furthest reaches. A large pond at the entrance is home to hundreds of waterfowl. Adjacent to it, two smaller ponds are stocked with rainbow trout, many an arm's length in size. Used to being fed by visitors, the fish will gather expectantly at your feet.

Headquarters Conservation Area
SUE LEBRECHT

GUIDE NOTES

Location
From Hwy 9 at Clifford, turn north on County Rd 10 and continue 6 km north of Neustadt and follow signs.

Open
Daily.

Cost
$2 per person, payable in an honour box.

Facilities
The Wilderness Shop, run by the Friends of the Saugeen, open weekends 1 to 4:30 pm, rents snowshoes and sells food for fish and bird feeding. Heated outhouses, gift shop.

Rentals
Snowshoes $4 adults, $2 children.

Events
Laneways, trails and buildings throughout the park are lit with lights and candle lanterns during Christmas in the Country, an activity-filled event that includes bird-box building workshops and gingerbread-man decorating.

Tips
Bring your toboggan and ride the thrilling hills of Allan Park Conservation Area, 10 km away. Allan also offers extensive, trackset cross-country ski trails. From Headquarters, turn left and proceed to the first stop sign. Turn left, drive two concessions and turn right on

Concession 2, a gravel road, and continue 2 km.

Tourism Info
Grey-Bruce Tourism,
800-265-3127 or 519-371-2071,
gbta@osicom.net,
www.visitontario.com.

More Info
Saugeen Valley Conservation Authority,
519-364-1255,
fax 519-364-6990,
svca@bmts.com web,
www.svca.on.ca.

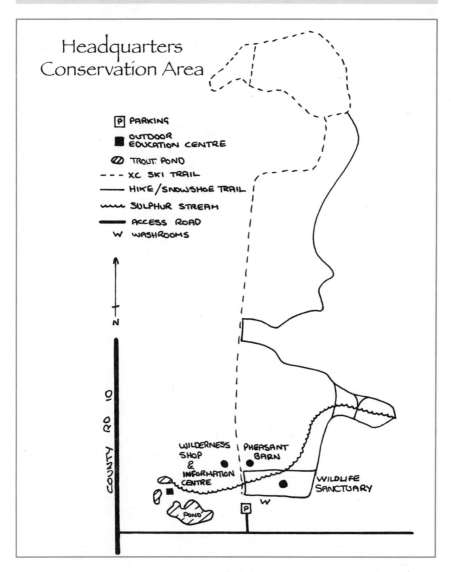

Headquarters
Conservation Area

P PARKING
■ OUTDOOR EDUCATION CENTRE
◍ TROUT POND
- - - XC SKI TRAIL
——— HIKE/SNOWSHOE TRAIL
∿∿∿ SULPHUR STREAM
━━━ ACCESS ROAD
W WASHROOMS

N

COUNTY RD 10

WILDERNESS SHOP & INFORMATION CENTRE

PHEASANT BARN

WILDLIFE SANCTUARY

POND

P   W

25   TALISMAN RESORT
Kimberley

❅   alpine ski and snowboard
❅   ski board
❅   cross-country ski
❅   tube
❅   snowshoe
❅   take a snowmobile tour
❅   dog sled
❅   horseback ride

Highlight: A buffet of activities
Impression: A splurge

Snowsport Mania
In the pretty, rural outback of Beaver Valley, Talisman is an upscale resort with a posh hotel on the slope of the Niagara Escarpment. Foremost, it caters to alpine skiers and snowboarders, with 18 trails, including an elaborate terrain and snowboard park.

For alternative thrills, it offers rentals of ski boards and sled dogs. The boards are 80- to 100-centimetre-long mini-skis with upturned tips and tails. Easy to learn, fun to use, they offer agility to carve, jump, perform 360-degree turns and do tricks in the halfpipe. Sled dogs are flat-bottomed boots with metal edges and curled up toes that allow you to "skate" down the hill.

With a vertical drop of 180 metres, Talisman's trails are wide and well groomed. Most start with steep upper lip and end with a long gradual bottom. There are segregated beginner and kids' areas, making this a good place for beginners.

Adrenaline Alley, at the resort's south end, is an 18-storey-high tubing park with nine chutes, serviced by two lifts. Enhanced by music and lit at night, the chutes, when slick from use, promote speeds of up to 50 kph. Grab a tube, ride the lift, pick a chute, buddy up and prepare to scream. But before you go, visit the bathroom in the base lodge, as there's not one at the park.

The resort also offers a 10-km network of groomed and trackset cross-country ski trails, snowshoeing on the Bruce Trail—which runs through the property—and snowmobile tours, and dog sledding and horseback riding on request through local outfitters.

GUIDE NOTES

Location
From Hwy 400, take Hwy 89 west to Hwy 10 north, go 35 km to Flesherton, turn right at the lights and follow Grey County Rd 4 (formerly Hwy 4) east for 2 km to Grey County Rd 13 and go north for 11 km to Kimberley.

Open
Alpine daily 8:30 am to 4:30 pm. Tubing Fri nights, weekends, daily during Christmas holidays.

Cost
Lift tickets $35 adults, lower rates for children and seniors. Tubing $10 for 2 hours adults, lower rates for children and seniors.

Facilities
Base lodge with cafeteria, bar, Italian Buffet Brunch on Sundays. Hotel lodging with a fitness centre, hot tub, sauna, heated outdoor pool, nightly entertainment and fine dining.

Rentals
Equipment for all sports available. Ski equipment $23, snowboarding $30, ski boards $10 for 2 hours.

Events/Programs
Lessons, camps, beginner packages, numerous events for both alpine and snowboarding.

Tips
Bring winter boots for tubing.

Tourism Info
Georgian Triangle Tourist Association, 705-445-7722, geotri@georgian.net, www.georgiantriangle.org.

More Info
Talisman Resort, 800-265-3759 (hotel reservations) or 519-599-2520, www.talisman.ca.

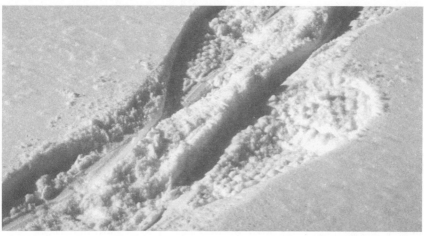

PINERY PROVINCIAL PARK

26 FESTIVAL OF NORTHERN LIGHTS
Owen Sound

❄ wander among lit animated displays
❄ ride horse-drawn wagons
❄ skate
❄ participate in kids' outdoor games, indoor crafts

When: Mid-Nov to mid-Jan
Highlight: Opening ceremonies with live music, a torchlight parade, carol singing, fireworks and more
Impression: A festive family getaway

Bright Lights, Sweet City

Santa is everywhere: in a hot-air balloon, under a spaceship, playing a guitar, sitting on a motorcycle and driving a school bus full of reindeer. Mickey Mouse and Minnie wave hello. Elvis sings. Snow White and the seven dwarfs return from the mine. Snoopy sits in the cockpit of a First World War Sopwith Camel plane.

Featuring over 250 displays and over 13 kilometres of light strings wound into trees along the banks of the Sydenham River, Owen Sound's Festival of Northern Lights attracts thousands of visitors.

Church bells chime and organ pipes play Christmas music as you follow lit walkways lined with displays on both sides of the river. A horse carousel turns in a bandshell, and you're lured to peer through windows of mini-houses. There are biblical scenes with angels, baby Jesus and Noah's Ark, as well as imaginative creations such as the fire-breathing sea serpent.

Everything, everywhere, is lit with colour, from ships and silos in the harbour, to residential homes, shops and streets. The scene is a twinkling kaleidoscope, and a display of community spirit.

Opening ceremonies, held on a Friday night, include live music, a torchlight parade, sleigh rides, clowns, carol singing and fireworks. Also, for the first two weekends, a children's festival is held in Harrison Park during daylight hours with hay rides, skating, outdoor games and indoor craft workshops. By night, thousands more lights are seen here. December 1999 marks the 12th year of the festival.

GUIDE NOTES

Location
Owen Sound city centre with lights and displays on 1st Ave W, 1st Ave E, and in Harrison Park.

Open
During the six-week-long festival, lights are on daily from 5 to 11 pm, with extended hours through Christmas week.

Cost
Free, but donations in on-site boxes appreciated.

Facilities
Plenty of parking.

Tips
Catch an afternoon Christmas performance at the Roxy before touring the lights, 519-371-2833.

Tourism Info
Owen Sound Tourism, 888-675-5555 or 519-371-9833, www.city.owen-sound.on.ca.

More Info
Festival of Northern Lights, 519-376-1440 ext 225.

27   SAUBLE BEACH CROSS-COUNTRY SKI TRAILS
Sauble Beach

❊   cross-country ski

Highlights: 20 km of trails through varied forested settings, deer sightings
Impression: An experience in tranquillity

Seductive Setting

From the heated chalet, where hot cider is served on weekends, head to the Rankin Dam to see a brook that rarely freezes. The approximately hour-long round trip travels over waves of hills through pine and spruce forest. From the dam, another hilly 10 kilometres brings you to a flat, sheltered area of maples and birches, so cozy you won't even feel the wind blow.

Well-marked with large maps at main intersections, this club-maintained, 20-kilometre trail system is groomed and single trackset in a succession of forested loops. For beginners there's a flat 5-kilometre circuit. For intermediates, there's Ruth's Ridge, a steep, narrow ridge at treetop level, with a deep valley to one side. White birch trickle down the slopes, and the descent—barely wide enough for a snowmobile to trackset—is long, slow and peaceful.

If you have two vehicles, park one at the chalet and the other at the start of Dawson Trail, about 5 kilometres north of the main entrance. Look for a sign on the east side of the road, and park on the shoulder. From there it's an easy up and down—mostly down—two-hour ski back to the chalet.

SAUBLE BEACH CROSS-COUNTRY SKI TRAILS

Sauble Beach Cross-Country Ski Trails

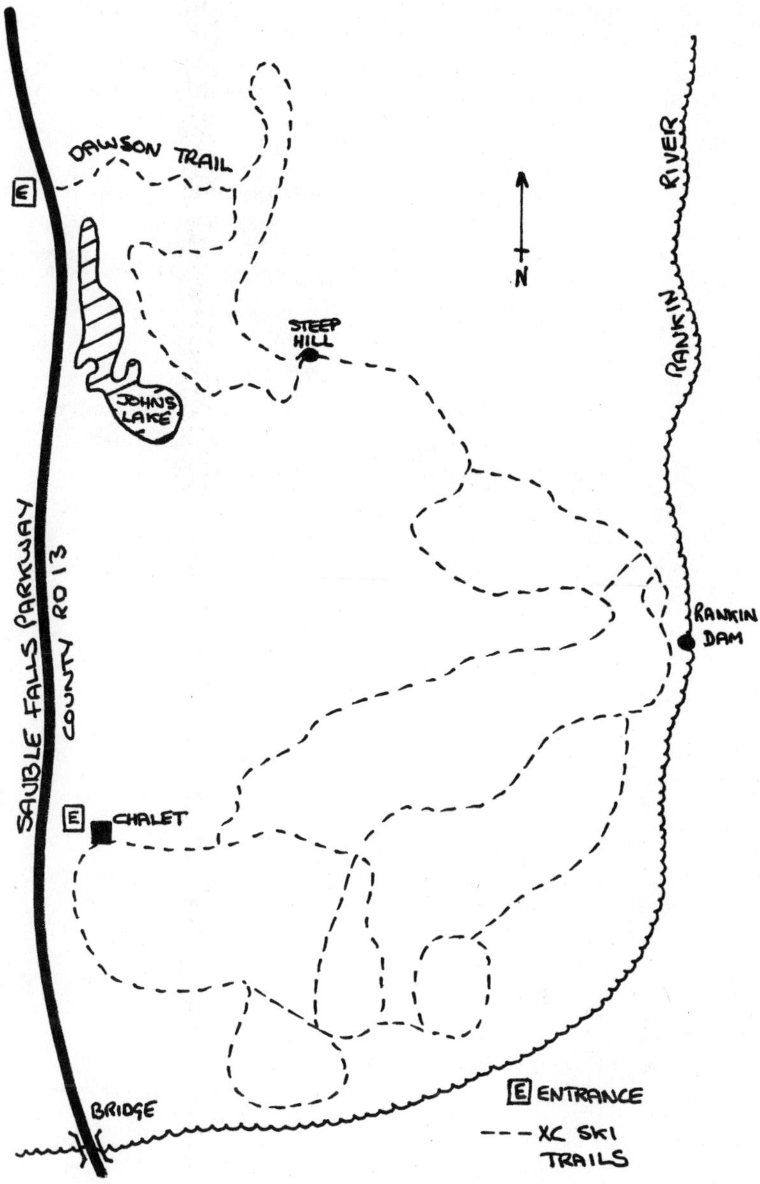

DAWSON TRAIL

E

STEEP HILL

JOHNS LAKE

N

RANKIN RIVER

RANKIN DAM

SAUBLE FALLS PARKWAY
COUNTY RD 13

E CHALET

BRIDGE

E ENTRANCE

--- XC SKI TRAILS

97

GUIDE NOTES

Location
In Sauble Beach, turn north at the traffic lights (there's only one set) and go 5.6 km on County Rd 13 (Sauble Falls Parkway) and park on the road shoulder just past the bridge over Rankin River. A sign marks the spot, and the chalet is a short hike in, on the east side of the road.

Open
Daily. The chalet is open only on weekends.

Cost
Trail passes are $4 single, $6 family. They can be purchased at the chalet on weekends and at Home Hardware on Main St in Sauble Beach on weekdays.

Facilities
Roadside parking, heated chalet with hot cider open weekends only, trail maps.

Rentals
None at the site, but nearby at Suntrail Outfitters in Hepworth on Hwy 6, 519-935-2478.

Tourism Info
Grey-Bruce Tourism, 800-265-3127 or 519-371-2071, gbta@osicom.net, www.visitontario.com.

More Info
Sauble Beach Cross-Country Ski Trails, 519-422-1405 or 519-422-3354.

LONDON/GRAND BEND

28   CIRCLE R RANCH
West of London

* ❄ cross-country ski
* ❄ skate-ski
* ❄ night ski

EVENTS
* Moonlight Dinner and Ski Tour: Sat closest to the full moon
* Day Camp for kids: March Break

Highlights: 20-km network through hills and valleys. Moonlight skiing.
Impression: When conditions are good, the experience is excellent.

Roller Coaster Circles

A top-of-the-line cross-country centre, Circle R Ranch unfortunately does not lie in a snowbelt and only manages to offer a maximum of eight weeks of skiing. Go when it snows and you'll be treated to a rollicking 20-km network of trails—all well-groomed, mapped, marked, colour-coded and unidirectional.

The rectangular-shaped property encompasses a plateau in the east, forested hills in the west, and a long valley of open fields in the south with the Dingman Creek snaking through it. A full circuit will take you through sugarbush and pine forest, up heart-thumping climbs, down deep gullies, on fast straightaways in wind-exposed fields, and along the pretty banks of the Dingman.

The Red and Blue main routes—the Red trackset for classical and the Blue groomed for skate-skiing—present a 5-kilometre-long course with optional shortcuts and an expert-rated extension. Beginners have a choice of two easy trails. Rentals are all up-to-date and the ski shop here has one of the largest selections of nordic equipment in Southern Ontario.

Night skiing is offered Thursday to Saturday on a 1.5-kilometre loop. For kids, a March Break Day Camp includes horseback riding, cross-country skiing—weather permitting—hay rides, crafts, games and more.

The moonlight ski event, limited to 60 people, includes dinner and an evening guided ski tour. Participants get a roast beef and chicken dinner or vegetarian fare with a salad bar, hot and cold beverages and dessert, before hitting the trails.

GUIDE NOTES

Location

8 km west of London. From Hwy 401, pass all the London exits and take Hwy 402 (towards Sarnia) to the Delaware/Melbourne Exit, go east to Delaware, then east on Hwy 2 to Carriage Rd (at Twin Streams Golf) and go north 2 km.

Open

Sun to Wed, 10 am to 5 pm, Thurs to Sat, 10 am to 10 pm.

Cost

Full-day/half-day trail passes are $6.50/$5 adults, $3.50/$3 ages 12 and under, $20/$16 family pass, under 5 free, seniors and students half-price weekdays.

Facilities

Heated main lodge with snack bar. Ski shop, open weekends only, 10 am to 5 pm or by appointment, 519-670-3447.

Rentals

Full day/half day are $22/$16 adults, $13/$11 children.

Events/Programs

Lessons. Moonlight Dinner and Ski Tour is $17 adults, $8.50 for ages under 12; preregistration required. March Break Children's Camp is for ages 6 to 13. Sleigh rides, group sugarbush tours.

Tourism Info

Tourism London, 800-265-2602 or 519-661-5000, fax 519-661-6160, webmaster@city.london.on.ca, www.city.london.on.ca.

More Info

Circle R Ranch, 519-471-3799, circlerranch@odyssey.on.ca, www.odyssey.on.ca/~circlerranch.

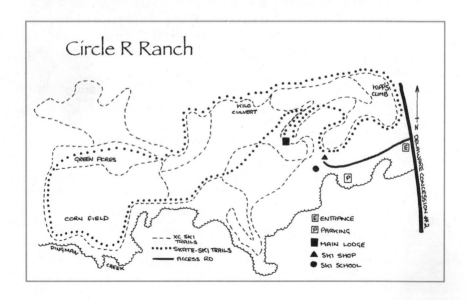

29 PINERY PROVINCIAL PARK
South of Grand Bend

* cross-country ski
* skate-ski
* toboggan
* skate
* hike
* walk the beach
* winter camp
* lodge in a yurt

EVENTS
* Nature programs: Weekends at 2 pm
* Christmas Sale and Tree Decorating: Dec 1 to 24
* Christmas Bird Count: Sun before Christmas
* Owl Prowl: Last Sat in Jan
* Stories in the Snow: Weekend in mid-Feb
* Return of the Swans: Last two weekends in March

Highlights: Watching the setting sun at the beach after a day of hiking, skiing and skating, before retiring into a cozy yurt.
Impression: A precious, well-rounded playground

Maximizing Momentum
Snow-covered sand dunes, an ice-covered river, and a beach with exploding ice volcanoes are set on fire each night by the setting sun on Lake Huron's horizon.

Packed trails for hiking and trackset trails for cross-country skiing are like roller coasters through the waves of dunes that escalate in height from a few metres at the beach to more than 30 metres at the park entrance. One sizable dune serves as a toboggan hill that's lit at night. An adjacent hollow, paved, flooded and frozen, provides an ice rink.

A boardwalk and staircase lead down to the beach—a 10-kilometre-long shoreline of pressure ridges and ice formations. Interpretive hikes and ski jaunts are offered every Saturday and Sunday at 2 pm. A comfort station with hot showers, toilets and laundry facilities helps encourage visitors to stay overnight at electrical and non-electrical sites, or in heated yurts that sleep up to six people in bunks.

Scoping the Setting

However you experience it, the Pinery is precious. It encompasses one of the largest areas of natural vegetation remaining in Southwestern Ontario. Its parallel series of dunes are host to oak savanna—a globally rare ecosystem. Fifty percent of the world's oak savanna lies in this park. Marram grass pokes through the snow near the beach, and sand cherry, bearberry, yellow puccoon, ground juniper, balsam poplar and oak thrive further inland, selectively decorating the rolling white mounds with life. Wintering birds flit among the shrubs and wiry branches.

For cross-country skiing there's a total of 38 kilometres of trails: four trackset loops plus an 11-kilometre out-and-back skate-skiing lane. For hiking, there are two looped, hard-packed trails, each with an accompanying booklet that provides ecological information about sites at numbered posts en route. The booklets range in price from 50¢ to $1.25, but are free if you return them to the box at the trailhead.

A chalet with heated washrooms and a wood-burning stove lies at the base of the toboggan hill, beside the skating rink. The four rental yurts, which get booked up early, are each equipped with a table and chairs, electric lighting and heating, a gas barbecue and picnic shelter. Besides its weekend interpretive programs, the park holds a number of special events.

Feathers and Flakes

Christmas Sale and Tree Decorating is a decorating program for children, in conjunction with the park's Nature Store's annual Christmas sale. During the Christmas Bird Count visitors assist with the "feeder survey" and learn to identify the common birds that come to the park's feeders. The Owl Prowl, an evening event limited to 50 participants, begins with an illustrated talk and ends with an evening hike, listening for the calls of nesting great horned owls. Stories in the Snow teaches animal track identification with a guided hike. And Return of the Swans highlights the spectacular tundra swan migration, with naturalists and volunteers providing spotting scopes and information on their natural history.

GUIDE NOTES

Location
Located 8 km south of Grand Bend on Hwy 21.

Open
Daily, 8 am to 10 pm.

Cost
Day pass $8 per vehicle. Ski passes are $2 adults, $1 ages 6 to 17.

Facilities
Visitors' Centre with nature exhibits and a gift shop, open daily, 1 to 4 pm and weekends 10 am to 4 pm. Firewood for sale.

Rentals
Cross-country ski equipment is available on weekends whenever the ski trails are open; full-day/half-day rentals are $12/$6 adults, $8/$4 children. Yurts rent for $40 to Mar 31; a $6 non-refundable reservation fee is extra.

Events/Programs
Christmas Sale and Tree Decorating, 519-243-1521. Owl Prowl, preregister, 519-243-8545.

Tips
The park only gets a small number of ski days—go when there's snow. Book early for yurts.

Cautions
Don't walk on the shoreline ice.

Tourism Info
Grand Bend Chamber of Commerce,
519-238-2001,
www.grandbend.com.

More Info
Pinery Provincial Park,
519-243-2220,
www.pinerypark.on.ca.

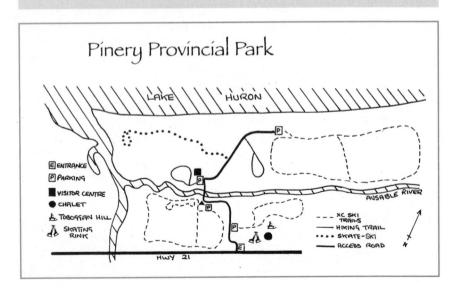

30 *SWAN MIGRATION,* OLD THEDFORD BOG
South of Grand Bend

❋ see swans by the thousands
❋ learn species identification
❋ watch mating rituals
❋ join guided hikes
❋ hear illustrated talks

When: Mid- to late March
Highlight: Swans flying so low you can hear their wings flap
Impression: A majestic spectacle

White Wings
Tundra swans by the thousands are expected on the Old Thedford Bog in Lambton County, near Grand Bend, in late March. On their northward migration from Chesapeake Bay in the state of Delaware to the breeding grounds of the Arctic tundra, massed flocks stop to rest and feed on remnants of corn crops at this Ontario location.

An estimated 10,000 of these majestic birds are seen here most years. Spread out on 20 kilometres worth of bog, they honk loudly in the early morning and at dusk, and fly back and forth so low you can hear their wings flap.

Pick up a map from the Lambton Heritage Museum or Pinery Provincial Park's Visitor Centre and follow a 3-kilometre driving tour to four viewing stations, where spotting scopes are set up in windbreak huts.

SUE LEBRECHT

105

On the last two weekends of March, naturalists are on site to point out different species and discuss their various behaviours.

The Museum highlights the spectacle with special events, including illustrated talks, naturalist-led hikes, and a live presentation of hawks and owls by the Tamarack Raptor Rehabilitation Foundation. Also on display is Paint the Huron Shores, an annual fine art competition featuring wildlife and landscape images of Southern Ontario. The Pinery features a 20-minute life-cycle film on swans, produced with local content.

In addition, numerous species of both diving and dabbling ducks, and possibly snowy owls, snow buntings and horned larks, can be seen on the flooded fields adjacent to the museum.

Before heading out, visit the Pinery's website to see a link that follows the swans' northward migration. Through the site you can also sponsor a swan to be tracked, and suggest a name for the next swan to be collared with radio telemetry equipment.

GUIDE NOTES

Location
Lambton Heritage Museum is located on the east side of Hwy 21, 8 km south of Grand Bend. Pinery Provincial Park is located on the west side of Hwy 21, 8 km south of Grand Bend.

Open
Museum is open daily from 11 am to 5 pm.

Cost
Viewing is free. Museum admission is $3.75 adults, $3 students/seniors, $1.75 children. The guided walk is $8; preregistration required.

Facilities
The Museum has rest rooms. For facilities at the Pinery, see page 104.

Events
Interpretive events are held on the last two weekends of March.

Tips
Bring binoculars. Also, see page 108 on Alymer Wildlife Management Area.

Tourism Info
Grand Bend Chamber of Commerce,
519-238-2001,
www.grandbend.com.

More Info
Lambton County Heritage Museum, 519-243-2600,
Swan Hotline, 800-265-0316,
Pinery Provincial Park,
519-243-8575,
www.pinerypark.on.ca.

31 *SWAN MIGRATION*, AYLMER WILDLIFE MANAGEMENT AREA
Southeast of London

❄ see swans by the thousands
❄ watch mating rituals

When: Mid- to late March
Highlight: Watching tundra swans up close
Impression: A loud and beautiful spectacle

Grace and Noise

The ugly duckling that turned into a princely white swan visits Aylmer Wildlife Management Area each spring, with an entourage of thousands.

During the last two weeks of March, about 140,000 migrating tundra swans pass through Western Ontario, stopping to rest and refuel at a number of sites. They're making their way diagonally across North America from their wintering site on the eastern seaboard of the United States to their breeding grounds in the Canadian high arctic.

At the wetland of Aylmer Wildlife Management Area, they arrive in waves of up to 2,000 birds a day. Corn is set out to attract the waterfowl, and three viewing stands—one of which is glass-enclosed, another wheelchair accessible—welcome visitors to watch the spectacle up close. Also, during the last two weekends in March, spotting scopes are usually set up.

The majestic birds, with their wide wingspan, land and take off all day long. Twice the size of Canada geese, they are pure white, except for black legs, feet and bills. Many will be courting, while others will be reinforcing their bonds. It's a loud affair. Swans making vows for life face each other, slowly extend and wave their wings, then bow their heads and sing a sequence of loud, melodic notes.

SUE LEBRECHT

GUIDE NOTES

Location
From Hwy 401, take Hwy 73 south and follow signs to the Ontario Police College. The wildlife area lies behind the college.

Open
Daily.

Cost
Free.

Facilities
Paved parking lot with three adjacent viewing stands. Outhouses are on the site during the migratory season. A refreshment booth may be set up.

Events
Spotting scopes are usually set up the last two weekends of March.

Tips
Morning is the best viewing time. Bring binoculars, and don't forget your camera. Also, see page 105 on Old Thedford Bog.

Tourism Info
Aylmer and District Museum and Tourist Centre, 519-773-9723.

More Info
Ministry of Natural Resources, Aylmer District, 519-773-9241, Swan Line, in operation from mid-March for three weeks, 519-773-7926.

Beamer Memorial Conservation Area
SUE LEBRECHT

NIAGARA/ST. CATHARINES

32 *HAWK MIGRATION,* BEAMER MEMORIAL CONSERVATION AREA
Grimsby

❋ watch birds of prey
❋ learn species identification
❋ hike trails
❋ gaze from lookout platforms

When: Late Feb to mid-May
Highlights: Watching big birds, up close. Hiking on the edge of the Niagara Escarpment
Impression: The beginning of a contagious hobby

Eye Spy
Look up to see hawks, eagles, falcons and vultures, passing as low as 15 metres overhead. An average of 13,000 birds of prey soar past this park annually from late February to mid-May, during their spring migration. On a good day, with mild temperatures, few clouds, and a wind from the south or southeast, you can see hundreds an hour.

Traditionally, peak periods are the end of March and the third week of April. During these periods, the Niagara Peninsula Hawkwatch group, which has been using this park as a counting site since 1975, presents free identification workshops, along with a one-day open house with various nature groups.

Early birds include the bald eagle and red-tailed hawk. By mid-March red-shouldered hawks pass by, then turkey vultures and golden eagles. Osprey arrive at the beginning of April, and broad-winged hawks appear near the month's end. Usually 14 species are seen, along with one or two rarities.

Flight Circuit
Coming from as far south as Argentina, the raptors are flying north, circling up warm currents of rising air called thermals, and gliding from one to the next with hardly a flap of their wings. As there is no thermal activity over water, most soar around the Great Lakes rather than over them, making the Niagara Peninsula a prime gateway.

SUE LEBRECHT

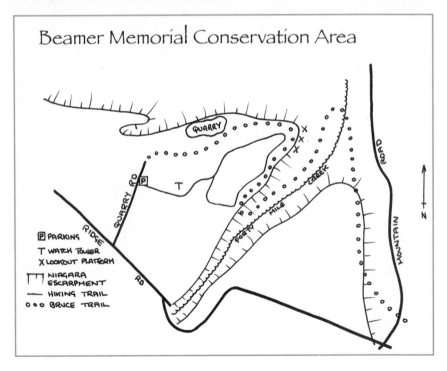

Beamer Memorial Conservation Area

QUARRY

RIDGE

QUARRY RD

FORTY MILE CREEK

MOUNTAIN ROAD

RD

N

P PARKING
T WATCH TOWER
X LOOKOUT PLATFORM
NIAGARA ESCARPMENT
HIKING TRAIL
o o o BRUCE TRAIL

A display board identifies the various birds and their characteristics, and a 6-metre-high watch tower stands in the middle of an open field. Trails through woods lead to three south-facing lookout platforms on the Escarpment's cliff edge.

Follow the red-blazed park trails through the naked forest to the white-blazed Bruce Trail, which hugs the edge of the Escarpment among old cedars. From the platforms you can see the straight streets of Grimsby stretching to Lake Ontario, the rising spray from Niagara Falls, and Forty Mile Creek with its deep valley.

GUIDE NOTES

Location
From the QEW near Grimsby, take Exit 71 and go south on Christie St for 2.6 km (it becomes Mountain Rd), turn right on Ridge Rd, go 1.5 km to Quarry Rd and turn right.

Open
Daily.

Cost
Free.

Facilities
Parking lot.

Events
The Niagara Peninsula Hawkwatch group presents free identification workshops late March to late April, weekends, 10 am to 3 pm, as well as an annual open house with various nature groups on Good Friday.

Tips
Bring binoculars, a lawn chair and lunch. Prime viewing time is between 10 am and 2 pm. Don't come in the rain.

Tourism Info
Grimsby & District Chamber of Commerce, 905-945-8319.

More Info
Niagara Peninsula Conservation Authority, 800-263-4760 or 905-227-1013, www.conservationlands.com.

33 *WINTER FESTIVAL OF LIGHTS,* NIAGARA FALLS
Niagara Falls

❄ light-seeing
❄ sight-seeing

EVENTS:
❧ Winter Festival of Lights: Third weekend of Nov to mid-Jan
❧ Ice Bridge: Forms most years

Highlight: Canada's largest light festival
Impression: Not just the Canadian capital of honeymoons, gambling and tacky museums

Bright Nights
When spray from the falls coats nearby lampposts, trees and railings with frost, when gigantic icicles form on either side of the giant cataract, and when the Winter Festival of Lights turns on, Niagara Falls transforms into an outdoor gallery.

More than 100 light displays, including 25 motion light displays with Disney characters, are set up along the Niagara Parkway, between Clifton Hill Road and the village of Chippawa. The main stage of pageantry is at Queen Victoria Park, a huge lawn in a backdrop of rock at the base of Murray Hill. Another concentration of displays lies on the Dufferin Islands, an intimate assembly of islands with bridges, south of the Greenhouse. Choose to walk or drive around.

The six-week-long showcase also includes fireworks over the falls and night parades with illuminated floats on select evenings. Not to be missed is Candles in the Park, a carolling concert in the outdoor Oakes Garden Theatre, where you'll stand among hundreds, singing old favourites, holding candles.

The city's Santa Claus parade just so happens to coincide with the festival's opening day. The falls, as always, are illuminated from 5 pm to midnight, and from late November to early January visitors can also catch the light festival taking place across the gorge on the American side.

Ice Site
An ice bridge forms most winters at the base of Niagara Falls. Created by ice floes that break from Lake Erie, tumble over the falls, and accumulate in the eddy near the *Maid of the Mist* docks, the structure grows. It can span the

NIAGARA FALLS VISITOR & CONVENTION BUREAU

river, shoreline to shoreline—a jagged jam of massive ice fragments with the crevassed appearance of a glacier.

Tourists used to walk on the bridge. For more than half a century, beginning in the mid-1800s, they ventured down into the gorge to cross the formation and stand on its edge, near the base of the thundering falls. But in 1912, without warning, the bridge broke and swept three people to their deaths. Since then, winter visitors have only been allowed to marvel at the phenomenon from above.

The ice bridge will never be as spectacular as it once was, however. During a thaw in 1938, high winds pushed such immense quantities of ice over the falls that a 150-foot-high ice wall formed, causing the collapse of the steel arched Honeymoon Bridge. Now a boom of logs upstream, across the mouth of the river, prevents such onrushes of ice.

GUIDE NOTES

Location
From the QEW, take Hwy 420 east, which turns into Roberts St, then continues south to Falls Ave and merges into the Niagara Parkway.

Cost
Display viewing is free, but donations are appreciated in various Loonie Barrels. Candles in the Park is $2 and includes a candle and candle holder.

Tips
Also, see page 117 on Niagara Parks Butterfly Conservatory.

Tourism Info
Niagara Falls, Canada Visitor & Convention Bureau, 800-563-2557, nfcvcb@niagara.com, www.tourismniagara.com.

More Info
Winter Festival of Lights, 800-563-2557 or 905-374-1616. Parks and ice bridge, Niagara Parks Commission, 905-356-2241, www.niagaraparks.com.

34 NIAGARA PARKS BUTTERFLY CONSERVATORY

Niagara Falls

❇ see 2,000 butterflies

Highlight: Glass-enclosed butterfly conservatory
Impression: Immersion in a tropical rain forest, surrounded by butterflies

Flutter By

The Niagara Parks Butterfly Conservatory features North America's largest free-flying butterfly collection, showcasing 50 different species from around the world in a 990-square-metre glass-enclosed conservatory.

Pathways wind through the building. A 6-metre-high waterfall serenades. Colourful wings flutter above your head, and the delicate creatures land on your shoulders. They rest on broad leaves, perch on passion flowers and feast on rotten fruit served on yellow dishes.

A $15-million self-funded project that opened in December 1996, the conservatory draws attention to the butterfly's vital role in the food chain. Video presentations and a multi-media exhibit room offer insightful information.

Fewer than 5 percent of all butterflies reach adulthood. They taste food with their feet and drink nectar from flowers with their proboscis—a tongue that is hollow like a drinking straw. Their antennae are used for feeling, hearing and smelling; they do not have noses and most don't have ears. Butterfly blood is brown, yellow and green.

GUIDE NOTES

Location
The conservatory is housed in the Niagara Parks Botanical Gardens on the Niagara Parkway, 9 km north of Niagara Falls. From the QEW, take Hwy 405, exit the Niagara Parkway and go south 3 km.

Open
Daily, 9 am to 5 pm (last tickets sold at 4:30 pm).

Cost
$7.50 adults, $3.75 ages 6 to 12, ages 5 and under free.

Facilities
Gift shop, café, interactive exhibit room, introductory video.

Events
March Break program with crafts and educational workshops for kids.

NIAGARA PARKS BUTTERFLY CONSERVATORY

Tips
Expect line-ups or avoid them through time-ticketing, available by advance reservation. Also, see page 115 on Niagara Falls.

Tourism Info
Niagara Falls, Canada Visitor & Convention Bureau,
800-563-2557,
nfcvcb@niagara.com,
www.tourismniagara.com.

More Info
Niagara Parks Butterfly Conservatory,
877-642-7275 or 905-358-0025,
fax 905-356-8448,
npinfo@niagaraparks.com,
www.niagaraparks.com.

SUE LEBR

WYE MARSH WILDLIFE CE

MIDLAND/PENETANGUISHENE

35 WYE MARSH WILDLIFE CENTRE
East of Midland

❊ watch swans
❊ cross-country ski
❊ snowshoe
❊ hike
❊ hand-feed chickadees
❊ dog walk

EVENTS
🐾 Kids' Day Camp: March Break
🐾 Sweetwater Harvest: Last weekend in March

Highlights: Hearing trumpeter swans, exploring a marsh
Impression: An activity-oriented nature experience

Nature Immersion

See over-wintering trumpeter swans, feed chickadees in the palm of your hand, visit the Wildlife Interpretation Centre display hall, try snowshoeing, and explore 13 kilometres of cross-country ski trails. A non-profit environmental education facility, Wye Marsh is committed to connecting people to nature, and promoting an understanding of the vital role wetlands play within the environment.

First don snowshoes—free with admission—and head to the trumpeter swan pond. Trails wind among trees and over boardwalks spanning frozen marsh, to an aerated pond that is home to as many as 60 swans. The grand white birds with their enormous wingspan honk and fly low overhead.

The trail may be well-trodden and hikeable to this point, but you'll appreciate having snowshoes further afield, following the extensive boardwalk, the long dyke, or the Woodland or Muskrat Trails. The centre offers 8 kilometres of looped routes in and around its marsh. Leashed dogs are welcome to tag along.

Bring unsalted sunflower seeds for the resident black-capped chickadees. They're so used to being fed, they'll find you in the forest and excitedly skip between overhead branches. Hold seeds in the flat palm of your hand and one by one they'll land to pick a treat.

121

Next, explore the cross-country ski trails that do-si-do between woods and clearings. Groomed, double trackset, and scattered with bird feeders, trails roam through open fields and forests of cedar, maple, hemlock, ash and poplar. Five loops range from 1.6 to 5 kilometres in length. Ideal for families, all are fairly flat, though you can expect a big hill on the Green Trail.

A March Break Day Camp for ages 6 to 12 includes cross-country skiing, snowshoeing, dog sledding and indoor games and activities. Sweetwater Harvest, a maple syrup festival, features guided walks, crafts, artisan demonstrations, music, horse-drawn wagon rides and historical costumed interpretation of maple syrup production.

GUIDE NOTES

Location
On Hwy 12, 5 km east of Midland.

Open
Daily, 10 am to 4 pm.

Cost
$5 per person.

Facilities
Wildlife Interpretation Centre with exhibits, washrooms, gift shop.

Rentals
Cross-country ski rentals are $8. Snowshoes, free with admission.

Programs
Jack Rabbit Cross-Country Ski Program for kids.

Tips
Bring unsalted sunflower seeds for the chickadees.

Tourism Info
Midland-Penetanguishene Tourism Hotline, 800-263-7745 or 705-526-7884.

More Info
Wye Marsh Wildlife Centre, 705-526-7809, wyemarsh@cryston.ca.

SUE LEBRECHT

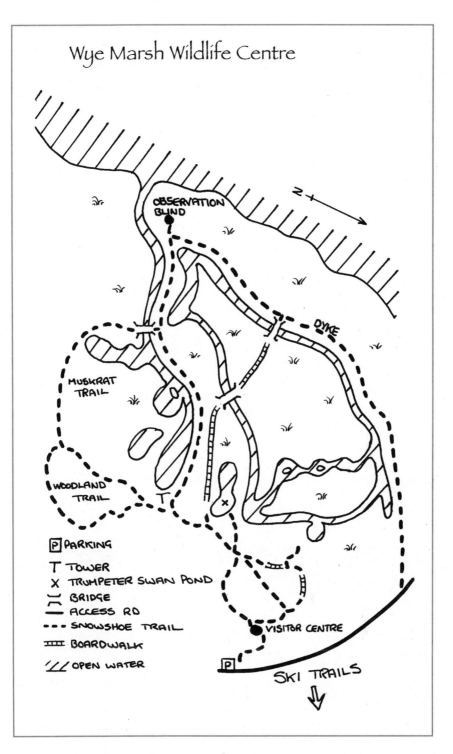

Wye Marsh Wildlife Centre

OBSERVATION BLIND

N

DYKE

MUSKRAT TRAIL

WOODLAND TRAIL

T

X

P PARKING
T TOWER
X TRUMPETER SWAN POND
BRIDGE
ACCESS RD
- - - SNOWSHOE TRAIL
BOARDWALK
/// OPEN WATER

VISITOR CENTRE

P

SKI TRAILS

36   LAFONTAINE SKI
West of Penetanguishene

❄ cross-country ski
❄ skate-ski

EVENTS
🍃 Moonlight skiing: Sat closest to the full moon

Highlights: Moonlight skiing. Ski and fish package.
Impression: An out-of-the-way, way-out ski site

Howl 'n' Ski
On Saturdays closest to the full moon, Lafontaine Ski opens its cross-country trails for use between 8 pm and midnight. You glide among shadows with a perception of speed—a safe yet eerie experience. Chili, bread, coffee and a fiddlin' step-dance await when you're done.

The resort offers 35 kilometres of trails in hilly hardwood forest. Unidirectional, mapped and colour-coded, the network consists of three double trackset loops, 2.5 to 15 kilometres in length, and a 7-kilometre-long skate-skiing loop.

One trail leads to a stocked trout pond, where—with prior arrangement and for a fee—you can cast a line and have your catch cleaned and barbecued for lunch while you wait in a heated cabin. Rod and bait are supplied.

The longest loop runs to the steep bluffs of Thunder Bay Lookout, with a view over Georgian Bay and islands. After soaking in the scenery, you can warm up in a nearby cabin, with a wood-burning stove and picnic table.

GUIDE NOTES

Location
From Hwy 400, Exit 89 in Barrie and take Hwy 27 north for 28 km to Simcoe Rd 6, go north 26 km to Simcoe County Rd 26 (also known as Concession 16), turn right and go 1.5 km.

Open
Daily, snow permitting. Sat closest to the full moon, 8 pm to midnight.

Cost
Trail fees are $9 adults, seniors and children 12 and under $6, family pass $25. Half-day rates available.

Facilities
Snack bar.

Rentals
Classic and skate-ski equipment available.

Tourism Info
Midland-Penetanguishene Tourism
Hotline, 800-263-7745
or 705-549-2232.

More Info
Lafontaine Ski, 705-533-2961,
www.lafontaine-ent.on.ca.

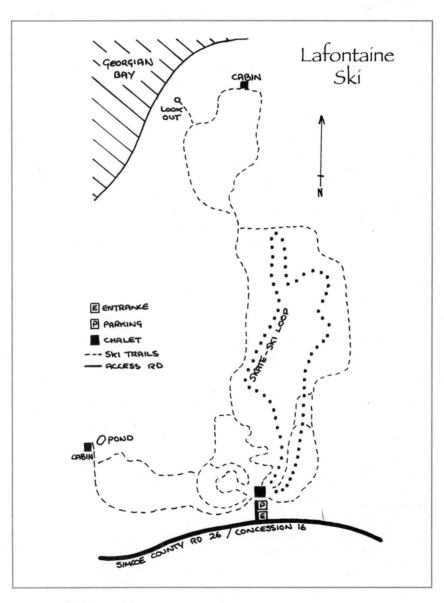

37 MOUNTAINVIEW SKI HILLS
Midland

❊ cross-country ski
❊ skate-ski
❊ alpine ski and snowboard

Highlight: 25 km of well-maintained cross-country trails
Impression: A quaint place to cruise on boards

Dual Board Vista
Mountainview features 25 kilometres of cross-country ski trails, double trackset with a groomed middle skate-skiing lane. As well, the centre has a small alpine hill with six runs, including a snowboard park on a wooded escarpment, serviced by two poma lifts.

Marked, colour-coded and unidirectional, trails form loops 1.5 to 10 kilometres in length. The Blue Trail streaks along the bottom of the escarpment. The Green extends through a golf course, zig-zagging among fairways, mounds and tree patches. The Red winds first through farm fields where pumpkins, strawberries and raspberries grow in summer. It then veers into rolling hardwood forest and climbs to the top of the alpine area, where you can see Blue Mountain's ski trails on the other side of Nottawasaga Bay.

GUIDE NOTES

Location
In Midland, from Hwy 93, turn west on Fosters Rd, between Mountainview Mall and the OPP Station.

Open
Daily for cross-country skiing, weekends only for alpine, 9 am to 4:30 pm.

Cost
Trail passes, $8 adults, $6 children, with rentals $12 and $10 respectively. Lift tickets, $14 adults, $10 children, with rentals $20 and $15 respectively.

Facilities
Chalet, rentals, pro shop, snack bar, washrooms.

Tips
Memorize the map board before heading out; there's no trail map to bring along. Make a weekend getaway of the Midland-Penetanguishene area and also visit the Wye Marsh Wildlife Area and Lafontaine Ski. The Best Western in Midland makes a good home base, 800-461-4265.

Tourism Info
Midland-Penetanguishene Tourism Hotline, 800-263-7745 or 705-526-7884.

More Info
Mountainview Ski Hills, 705-526-8149.

HUNTSVILLE/ALGONQUIN

38   MUSKOKA PIONEER VILLAGE
Huntsville

* skate
* tube
* tour a 19th-century heritage village

EVENTS
* Victorian Christmas: Second Sat before Christmas, 4 to 6 pm
* Winterfest: Last weekend in Feb and first weekend in March
* Maple Syrup Festival: March Break

Highlights: Pre-Christmas Victorian feast. Winterfest, when Cann Lake is surrounded by hundreds of candles
Impression: Enchanting skating anytime, but don't miss Winterfest

Old Fashioned Skating Party
Muskoka Pioneer Village features the largest outdoor skating arena in Muskoka—Cann Lake. Several rinks for hockey and pleasure skating are cleared, along with a speed-skating loop the size of a track-and-field oval. Overlooking it is a two-storey-high tubing hill, with tubes free for use.

But visit during Huntsville's annual Winterfest and experience the lake by night, aglow, encircled by hundreds of candles. The main stage for the town's festival, Cann Lake is also the site of a bed race, pond curling, pioneer challenges such as axe throwing and log sawing, and children's games including smooshing, where teams of four are each harnessed to two long boards. Dog sledders offer rides, and rink-side vendors provide hot chocolate.

Feasting Festivities
The village itself, a living history museum with 15 heritage buildings, comes alive during its Victorian Christmas and Maple Syrup Festival events.

Victorian Christmas is a roving feast, featuring early traditional dishes such as native fried fish and berries, trappers' wild game stew and bannock, English pigs in a blanket, and French tortiere. Families eat their way from one building to another—each decorated for a Victorian Yuletide and staffed by costumed interpreters.

There are candles in windows, wreaths on doors, handmade ornaments on Christmas trees and horse-drawn wagon or sleigh rides. Children make their own ornaments inside the schoolhouse, while a blacksmith demonstrates horseshoe-making and a native person talks about dream catchers and eagle feathers.

During the Maple Syrup Festival, visitors can see native and pioneer methods of maple syrup production, take horse-drawn wagon rides into the surrounding sugar bush, and indulge in syrup-smothered pancakes and sausages. "Trapper Bob" spins yarns of Muskoka's fur-trapping days, guided tours of the village are offered, and fiddling and bluegrass bands play on weekends.

GUIDE NOTES

Location
From Hwy 11, take Hwy 60 to the first set of traffic lights, turn right, go across the bridge, and turn left at the next set of lights onto Brunel Rd and go 2 km.

Open
Ice skating and tubing anytime, weather permitting.

Cost
Free.

Facilities
Outhouses, parking.

Rentals
Tubes free for use.

Events/Programs
Victorian Christmas and Maple Syrup Festival, $11 adults, $9 ages 6 to 12, ages 5 and under free, $30 families; reservations not required—just show up. Winterfest $5. Custom-organized group functions available.

Caution
A flag system indicates ice conditions. Yellow is safe. Red is not.

Tourism Info
Muskoka Tourism,
800-267-9700 or 705-689-0660,
fax 705-689-9118,
info@muskoka-tourism.on.ca,
www.muskoka-tourism.on.ca.

More Info
Muskoka Pioneer Village,
705-789-7576,
village@muskokapioneervillage.org,
www.muskokapioneervillage.org.

39   ARROWHEAD PROVINCIAL PARK
North of Huntsville

* cross-country ski
* skate-ski
* learn to ski
* tube
* snowshoe
* ice fish
* skate

Highlights: Extensive skiing, a tubing ravine, evening skating
Impression: Not just a playground for locals and cottagers, but a destination site for all

Muskoka Meanderings

Arrowhead Provincial Park near Huntsville features 27 kilometres of track-set trails, including 11 kilometres of groomed skate-skiing track, along with up-to-date rental equipment and lessons by certified instructors.

The trail network is comprised of eight loops that fan out from two separate parking lots, each with a warming hut. Loops range from 2.7 to 4.5 kilometres in length, but a couple are interconnected, to provide longer, more challenging excursions.

Among the trails, the rugged Beaver Meadow Loop includes a boardwalk stretch through frozen swamp. Arrowhead Lake offers a lake circumnavigation with bright vistas through different tree covers. The East River leads along a flat ridge to Big Bend Lookout, aptly named for the river's tight curve below and its surrounding crescent of sandy bluffs. At the loop's far end is Stubb's Falls, a dainty site of crystal-clear flow among snow-topped boulders fringed with ice.

Arrowhead also has a snowshoe trail, a 180-metre-long tubing ravine—but no uphill tow—an artificial skating rink, and allows ice fishing in two lakes, one stocked with speckled trout.

GUIDE NOTES

Location
Off Hwy 11, 8 km north of
Huntsville.

Open
Daily, 8 am to 5 pm.

Cost
$10 per vehicle. Cross-country trail
passes are $2 adults, $1 children.

Facilities
Warming huts, outhouse.

Rentals
Cross-country equipment $19; use
of tubes is free.

Programs
Lesson packages.

Tips
Nearby accommodations include
the budget Tulip Motor Inn and
Arrowhead Motor Inn and the five-
star-rated resorts of Grandview and
Deerhurst.

Tourism Info
Muskoka Tourism,
800-267-9700 or 705-689-0660,
fax 705-689-9118,
info@muskoka-tourism.on.ca,
www.muskoka-tourism.on.ca.

More Info
Arrowhead Provincial Park,
705-789-5105.

40   ALGONQUIN PROVINCIAL PARK
Northeast of Huntsville

❋   cross-country ski
❋   snowshoe
❋   dog sled
❋   see natural and human history exhibits
❋   winter camp
❋   lodge in a yurt or rustic cabin
❋   rent an electrical camping site
❋   participate in a multi-day, multi-adventure with tour operators

Highlights: Skiing past a frozen marsh and seeing moose tracks, plus the beast that made them
Impression: Serenity in all that you do

Adventure Buffet
What's your pleasure? Cross-country skiing? Algonquin Provincial Park offers three separate looped networks. Snowshoeing? Pick any one of a dozen trails. Dog sledding? Commercial operators provide guided tours at three locations. Want it all? Two outfitters offer multi-day adventures running the gamut.

Stay awhile—there are yurts and rustic cabins for rent. There are car-accessible plowed sites, with and without electrical hook-up, and interior backcountry camping is permitted. Nights are bright with stars. Trees crack like rifle shots in the frozen stillness, and the howl of wolves raises the hair on the back of your neck.

First stop is the Visitor Centre, offering not just user-friendly information on the park, but outstanding exhibits. Stroll among the nine life-size dioramas featuring the park's birds and animals. Trace the human influence on the park over time through archival photographs, a talking mannequin, and videos with old footage. Browse geological displays. Soak in appreciation for Ontario's oldest provincial park before heading out to play.

Algonquin presents easily accessible wilderness immersion. From the park's West Gate to its East Gate, the 56-kilometre-long corridor of Highway 60 is kept plowed and sanded all winter. The park's winter brochure provides detailed maps of its trails, with sectional distances, area descriptions, terrain challenges and notes of caution.

The three stacked-loop ski systems—providing a total of 80 kilometres —are all groomed and unidirectional, and nearly half are trackset. Wood-stove-heated shelter cabins and outhouses are available en route. For dog

HEAVEN

sledding, the park has three designated trails, including a 22-kilometre-long linear route that traces an old logging road. Snowshoe trails, ranging from one to 11 kilometres in length, trace summer hiking trails and are well-marked loops. For winter camping expeditions, trekkers can also follow either of the park's looped backpacking trails, or—for experienced winter waterway travellers—a specially-designed 8-kilometre out-and-back route that links a succession of lakes and creeks.

For a sheltered night in the wilderness, backcountry ski or snowshoe to the old rustic ranger cabins at Kitty and McKaskill Lakes, respectively 5 and 11 kilometres distant from the Shall Lake access point, north of the town of Madawaska. The cabins sleep eight and four people in bunks and have stoves for cooking.

The park's seven rental yurts, which are tent-like structures equipped with basic furniture and electrical heat, are all accessible by vehicle in the Mew Lake Campground, where plowed and electrical hook-up camp sites are also available.

Multi-Day Play

Two outfitters offer multi-day adventures in the park, both providing transportation from Toronto, food and all required equipment. Voyageur Quest, based in an authentic log cabin in the park, offers Footsteps of the Pioneer, an award-winning package that includes dog sledding, igloo building, backcountry skiing, snowshoeing and traditional pioneer meals. Call of the Wild offers three days of dog sledding, cross-country skiing and snowshoeing, with overnights in a lodge or hostel, as well as multi-day dog-sled expeditions and winter camping trips.

Overall, what to expect? Rolling hardwood forest and snow-covered lakes ringed by conifers. Birds, including ravens, gray jays, boreal chickadees,

PINERY PROVINCIAL PARK

crossbills, three-toed woodpeckers and spruce grouse. Animal tracks and chance sightings of deer, moose, marten, fisher, otter, fox and wolves. And foremost, serenity.

GUIDE NOTES

Location
The park can be accessed through its West or East Gate on Hwy 60.

Open
Daily. Traditionally, Algonquin starts gathering snow by late Nov and keeps it into early April.

Cost
Admission $10 per vehicle per day. Camping $10.25, or $13.25 with electricity.

Facilities
Visitors' Centre with exhibits, information, washrooms, a theatre, viewing deck, restaurant and bookstore, open weekends only Nov through April, 10 am to 5 pm. (Open to groups during the week.) Firewood for sale. There are 131 winter camp sites, electrical hook-up sites, 7 electrically heated yurts, 2 rustic cabins.

Rentals
Yurt and cabin rentals start from $55 per night; reservations required. Complete outfitting is available at Algonquin Outfitters, 705-635-2243.

Programs
Dog sledding, High Tundra Kennels, 705-635-2247, Chocpaw Expeditions, 705-386-0344, chocpaw@onlink.net, Algonquin-Way Kennels, 613-332-4005 or 613-332-1396, mush@northcom.net.

Multi-Adventures
Voyageur Quest, 416-486-3605 or 800-794-9660, voyquest@inforamp.net, www.inforamp.net/-voyquest/, Call of the Wild, 800-776-9453 or 416-200-9453, adventure@call-wild.com, www.call-wild.com.

Tips
Bring your own water.

Cautions
Never cross lakes or creeks without testing ice surfaces. Areas near creek mouths can be unsafe, even during the coldest weather. Always tell somebody where you're going and for how long. Carry a first aid kit, waterproof matches, spare socks and wool mittens, an extra sweater, a spare ski tip, electrical tape, and small piece of wire or nylon cord to repair poles or bindings. Temperatures may go down to minus 40 degrees Celsius at night.

More Info
Algonquin Provincial Park, 705-633-5572. Yurt and cabin reservations, 888-668-7275.

HALIBURTON/BANCROFT

41 HALIBURTON FOREST AND WILDLIFE RESERVE
South of Algonquin Provincial Park

❄ snowmobile
❄ watch wolves
❄ dog sled
❄ ice fish
❄ join various outdoor programs

EVENTS
🐺 Poker Ride: Third Sat in Feb

Highlights: 300 km of sledding trails through wilderness. Wolf Centre housing a pack of wolves
Impression: A snowmobiling wonderland. A howling education.

It's a Gas
Attracting 500 sledders on any given weekend day, Haliburton Forest, the only privately owned snowmobiling operation in North America, is a 50,000-acre wilderness with 300 kilometres of groomed trails.

The well-marked and mapped network consists of wide main routes and narrow secondary corridors that interconnect in loops through hardwood forest, around lakes, over hills, along ridges, to lookouts, icefalls and half a dozen lakeside warming huts.

Seeing the gorge is a must. It features a spectacle of 12-metre-long icicles hanging along the breadth of an escarpment. En route, ascend to Redstone Vista for a view to the south, up to the Lookout for a view to the north, and to Little Black Lake to see the quintessential frozen cascade.

Hilly, and strewn with 50 lakes and numerous ponds and creeks, this sledding playground has no road crossings, towns or dumps. Routes all roam dry land, and only some secondary trails offer optional lake crossings —staked, when safe, with fluorescent flagged poles.

Canis Lupus
Haliburton Forest is also home to the Wolf Centre, a 15-acre enclosure housing a pack of wolves. From the enclosed observation deck with one-way

windows there's a good chance you'll see them, padding up a hill, sitting on a rock, curled under a tree.

The centre also offers movies on wolves, including one on wolf myths. Examining folklore, from aboriginal reverence of the wolf to its portrayal as the European symbol of evil, the documentary shows how many people's perception of the wolf now bears little resemblance to the real thing. Egyptian, Inuit and Native Canadian wolf depictions hang on the wall, and there are jaw bones and fur to touch, wolf stories to read, and interactive computer games to play.

GUIDE NOTES

Location
At the end of Kennisis Lake Rd (Hwy 7), north of West Guildford.

Open
Daily. Wolf Centre is open Fri to Sun, 10 am to 5 pm.

Cost
Snowmobiling permit fee is $18 per day per person. Ages 18 and under ride free with an accompanying adult. Admission to the Wolf Centre is $5 adults, $3 for ages under 18.

Facilities
Restaurant, convenience store, lodging in rooms and housekeeping units.

Rentals
Double-seater snowmobile rentals are $120 per day midweek and $140 per day weekends; reservations and driver's licence required. Complete outfitting of boots, suits and helmets is also available.

Events/Programs
The Poker Ride is a big annual fundraiser for the local hospital. Call for various special outdoor nature-oriented programs.

Tourism Info
Haliburton Chamber of Commerce, 800-461-7677.

More Info
Haliburton Forest and Wildlife Reserve, 705-754-2198, fax 705-754-1179, halforest@halhinet.on.ca, www.haliburtonforest.com.

42 *SLED DOG DERBY*, MINDEN
Minden

❋ watch sled dog races
❋ cheer from grandstands
❋ chat with mushers from around North America

When: Mid-Jan
Highlights: The dog frenzy that precedes each race
Impression: Canada's largest sled dog race; a spectacle for dog lovers

Bow Wow

Harnessed to a sled, bursting with anticipation, teams of four and eight hyper dogs howl, leap, whine and yap. From the start on Main Street in Minden—which is closed to traffic—teams are released at two-minute intervals on four- and eight-mile courses in a race against the clock.

Spectators line the street and fill the tiered grandstands. On the word go from their masters, the dogs belt down the snow-covered road before veering into the bush. You see them struggling up a long steep climb with their mushers pushing from behind, then within a half hour to an hour—depending on the course—you'll see the same teams, now exhausted, tongues dangling, racing down a wide lane towards the finish.

Featuring one of the most challenging courses on the Canadian circuit, testing both stamina and driving skills, Minden attracts more than 50 mushers, with teams from as far away as Alaska and California. January 2000 marks the 16th annual derby.

MINDEN TIMES

Before, after, and in between races, spectators are welcome to visit the pits and talk to the mushers. The event also includes an ultra-cute Kid and Mutt Race.

GUIDE NOTES

Location
Minden is three hours northeast of Toronto on Hwy 35.

Cost
Free for spectators.

Facilities
Outdoor sausage vendors, restaurants, dinners at churches.

Tips
Reserve accommodation well in advance.

More Info
Haliburton Chamber of Commerce, 800-461-7677.

SUE LEBRECHT

138

43   HALIBURTON HIGHLANDS
Haliburton

❄ cross-country ski
❄ skate-ski
❄ ski lodge-to-lodge
❄ night ski

Highlight: Ontario's most extensive cross-country ski trail network
Impression: trackset trails in the wilderness for serious enthusiasts

Vast Strokes
As you ski among towering hardwoods, cross bridges over streams and climb to hilltops affording vistas of white lakes and endless forest, you may not spot another soul. The Haliburton Highlands, a hilly wooded plateau spotted by lakes, features Ontario's most extensive cross-country ski network, with more than 80 kilometres of connected loops.

Maintained by the Haliburton Nordic Trails Association, trails are double trackset, intersections are posted with numbers that correspond to a trail map, and three shelter cabins provide warm-up lunch spots. Access is through the Haliburton Museum and 12 different lodging properties that link directly to the system. Passes are sold at each resort, hotel and inn, and at the museum. Many properties have rental equipment, some offer lessons, and a few will even provide multi-day lodge-to-lodge packages, with luggage transfers on request. But for the most part, visitors tend to base themselves at any one of the properties and make out-and-back excursions.

The largest concentration of trails lies in the cradle of Lake Kashagawigamog—site to five lodging properties. There's the easy 6-kilometre Slipper Loop, the expert 12-kilometre Olympic Loop and the 11-kilometre Jim Beef Trail, which is also groomed for skate-skiing. A portion of the Olympic Loop provides a gateway to trails running north and west, while the Jim Beef Trail leads east to the easy 5-kilometre Glebe Park Loop, which has a nature interpretation section as well as a 2-kilometre night-lit circle.

You can ski for a week without doing the same trail twice. Accommodation ranges from quaint country cabins to full-service resorts complete with indoor pools and horse-drawn sleigh rides. Prices range from $65 for a room to $165 for a private cottage with a fireplace and jacuzzi, plus two meals.

SUE LEBRECHT

GUIDE NOTES

Location
Hwy 35 to Hwy 121, go east 24 km to Haliburton Village. To reach the museum, turn left at the only stop lights in town, go 2 km north and turn left on Bayshore Acres Rd.

Open
Daily, with night skiing at Glebe Park.

Cost
Trail passes $9 adults, $6 students, children under 12 free with an adult.

Facilities
Three en-route warming huts, lodging.

Rentals
Cross-country equipment available from some lodging properties.

Events/Programs
Active seniors' club and Jackrabbit Program.

Tips
Lodge-to-lodge skiing is for strong skiers only.

Tourism Info
Haliburton Chamber of Commerce, 800-461-7677.

More Info
Haliburton Nordic Trails Association, 705-457-1640, or contact a resort directly. Resorts around Lake Kashagawigamog: Wigamog Inn 800-661-2010, Pinestone Inn 800-461-0357, Bonnie View 800-461-0347, Halimar 800-223-7322, Willow Beach Cottages 800-656-9067, Lakeview Motel 705-457-1027.

44   SILENT LAKE PROVINCIAL PARK
South of Bancroft

❊   cross-country ski
❊   skate-ski
❊   snowshoe
❊   winter camp
❊   stay overnight in a yurt
❊   rent a lodge for a group

EVENTS
❧   Saturday-night skiing on lantern-lit trails with headlamps

Highlight: A 19-km, long-distance challenge
Impression: An adventuresome outpost, for romance or a group party

Yurting to Ski
The yurt for rent at Silent Lake Provincial Park is a cozy abode. Set in the wilderness, a two-kilometre ski-in from the parking lot, the Mongolian-designed shelter is like a glorified tent.

Round, with a peaked roof, it's heated by a wood-burning stove. Its floor and canvas shell are insulated. A propane stove sits on a hutch full of pots and utensils against the lattice wall. In the middle, a small table is set with two chairs. Three windows and a central skylight let in light by day; candles brighten the interior by night.

It sleeps six on two bunks, the bottoms of which pull out into double beds. For $75 a night, it comes with a barrel of water and a stack of wood. An outhouse lies a five-minute walk or two-minute ski away.

Skiing 'til it Yurts
Starting from the lakeside parking lot, which is packed with cars most weekends, Silent Lake offers four trackset cross-country ski loops, 3, 6, 13 and 19 kilometres in length, plus a groomed 8-kilometre skate-skiing trail.

The longest loop is a commitment requiring good physical condition. From the 6-kilometre mark to its end, there's no shortcut or way out. The minimum two-hour, one-way route follows a series of beaver ponds through hardwoods, cedar swamps, groves of white birch, beech and hemlock. The way isn't difficult—there are no big hills, merely successions of little dips—but the distance can be gruelling.

At the 8-kilometre mark there's a 240-metre-long boardwalk built over a stream and swamp linking Silent Lake to Quiet Lake. At the 12-kilometre mark there's a welcoming warming hut equipped with a wood stove and firewood.

For snowshoeing, an 8-kilometre marked trail leads to Bonnie's Pond. Winter camping is available at sites located a one-km ski-in from the parking lot. And groups, to a maximum of 14, can rent the park's former staff house—a lodge with seven rooms, showers, a lounge and kitchen.

GUIDE NOTES

Location
On Hwy 28, 24 km (15 miles) north of Apsley and 25 km (15.5 miles) south of Bancroft.

Open
Daily, mid-Dec to the end of March, as snow conditions permit.

Cost
$7.50 per vehicle. Trail passes $2 adults, $1 kids and seniors. Yurts rent for $75 a night.

Facilities
Outhouses, picnic facilities, warm-up shelters. Rental yurt, rental lodge, winter campsites, firewood for sale.

Rentals
Cross-country equipment $20 per day, $15 per half day. Snowshoes $15 per day, $10 per half day. Headlamps $8.

Events
Sat night is always an event with lantern-lit trails, headlamp rentals and a bonfire, hot chocolate and sing-alongs.

Tips
Book the yurt months in advance.

Cautions
Don't ski past the boardwalk unless you're a strong skier, and bring water and snacks.

Tourism Info
Bancroft & District Chamber of Commerce, 613-332-1513, fax 613-332-2119, chamber@commerce.bancroft.on.ca, www.commerce.bancroft.on.ca.

More Info
Silent Lake Provincial Park, 613-339-2807 or 800-481-2925, reservations 888-668-7275, www.ontarioparks.com.

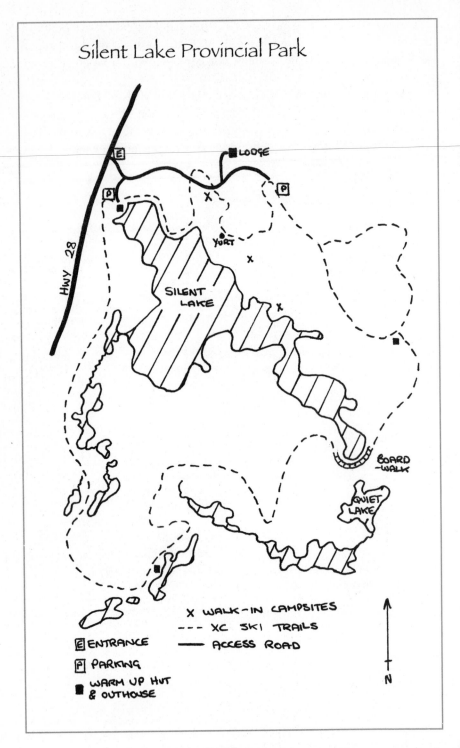

Silent Lake Provincial Park

X WALK-IN CAMPSITES
- - - XC SKI TRAILS
—— ACCESS ROAD

E ENTRANCE
P PARKING
■ WARM UP HUT & OUTHOUSE

EAST

BELLEVILLE/TRENTON

45   PRESQU'ILE PROVINCIAL PARK
South of Brighton

❄   see thousands of ducks, geese and swans
❄   join guided hikes
❄   witness exploding ice volcanoes
❄   cross-country ski
❄   winter camp

EVENTS
⚓ Christmas at Presqu'ile: First two weekends in Nov
⚓ Winterfest: Last weekend of Jan
⚓ Waterfowl Festival: Weekends in late March and early April

Highlights: Huge numbers and a rich variety of waterfowl, erupting ice hummocks
Impression: You don't need to be a birder to appreciate the spectacle of thousands of waterfowl

Fowl Spying
Presqu'ile Provincial Park is host to one of Ontario's great natural wonders. In early spring, tens of thousands of ducks, geese and swans descend on the wetland peninsula to rest and feed during their migration from Chesapeake Bay to the northern prairies and tundra.

The males are very energetic trying to attract a mate with a show of their vigour and brilliant plumage. Males circle around a single female, fighting with one another for attention. Each species has its own ritual of gestures and body movements. The bufflehead bobs its head rapidly. The common goldeneye stretches its neck, horizontally then skyward.

The majority of the approximately 25 different waterfowl species are not typical to Ontario and can only be seen here during their migration. Among the species found are the redhead, the near-goose-sized canvasback with its long sloping forehead, the scaup, named for the sound it makes, and old-squaws, which chatter constantly.

To highlight the spectacle, the park features an annual Waterfowl Festival, with viewing scopes on duck trucks—specially constructed mobile platforms with wind and rainproof roofs and walls. Set in three to five different

locations, the stations are manned by volunteer naturalists who help with identification and explain courtship behaviour. Attracting 9,000 people, the event includes a waterfowl carving display and children's activities.

Frosty Festivities
Among other annual events, Christmas at Presqu'ile is a fine arts and crafts show and sale, and Winterfest is a community-based festival. While the town of Brighton presents picnic activities with a twist, including a three-legged race on skis, outdoor curling using duck decoys, and a tug o' war in snow, the park features slide presentations on wintering birds, guided hikes, and a children's birdhouse building workshop.

Eruptions and Meanderings
The park's 10-kilometre-long peninsula is also the site of a formation of ice volcanoes. When shallow water freezes around the shoreline, incoming waves can no longer wash up on the beach. They ricochet off the ice wall and punch upwards through weak spots in the frozen surface, frothing like lava from a volcano. These spots grow with each eruption, forming hummocks up to 6 metres high.

Visit on a windy day, and bring your camera to snap the explosions. The higher the waves, the more spectacular the eruptions. Also, bring your cross-country skis and explore the park's 16 kilometres of marked, but ungroomed trails that roam forests and fields. Expect to see chickadees, waterfowl, cardinals and woodpeckers, along with a variety of animal tracks. Winter camping is allowed, but comfort stations aren't open, and no water is available, although firewood is for sale.

GUIDE NOTES

Location
From Hwy 401, take Hwy 30 south to Hwy 2, turn west and go 1 km to Ontario St, turn south and go 2 km to the gates.

Open
Daily, 7 am to 10 pm.

Cost
Per vehicle, $2 per hour, $4 per 2 hours, $7 per day at a self-serve fee station.

Facilities
Lighthouse interpretive centre is often open, noon to 4 pm. Indoor washrooms, outhouses.

Rentals
None.

Cautions
Do not walk on the ice. People have fallen through stress spots on the surface.

Tourism Info
Northumberland County Tourism, 800-354-7050 or 905-372-0141.

More Info
Presqu'ile Provincial Park, 613-475-4324, www.ontarioparks.com, www.friendsofpresquile.on.ca.

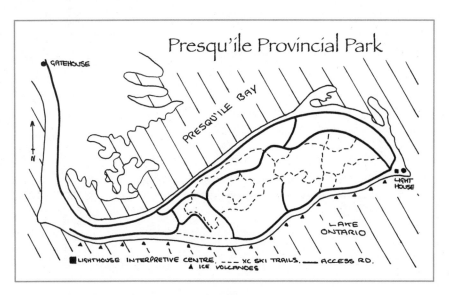

Presqu'ile Provincial Park

46   SANDBANKS PROVINCIAL PARK
South of Belleville

❄   cross-country ski
❄   see exploding ice volcanoes

Highlight: Cross-country skiing on a roller coaster of sand dunes
Impression: A beach blast on boards

Dune Strokes

Dunes, as high as 27 metres, a few actually covering old buildings, surround the Pannes, where water-filled depressions are frozen into a flat expanse. Sandy peaks jut from the snow, as do large pieces of driftwood, long grass and shrubs. Here, ski tracks peel away from the marked route and undulate like roller coasters among the mounds. Further ahead, the route runs to the shore of Lake Ontario, where 3-metre-high ice volcanoes can be seen erupting in high winds.

The park's 12-kilometre network criss-crosses a long sandbar dividing Lake Ontario from West Lake. From either of two parking lots, colour-marked trails first lead through sheltered pine plantation on a gently rolling course. Follow the Yellow Trail, the longest and most diverse of five options. Thanks to the Friends of Sandbanks, trails are trackset after each snowfall, and a ski chalet with a woodstove, one kilometre from the entrance, is kept supplied with wood and water.

SUE LEBRECHT

GUIDE NOTES

Location
From Hwy 401, take Hwy 33 south to Bloomfield, then go 15 km south on County Rd 12.

Open
Daily.

Cost
Free, but donations appreciated in a drop box at the ski chalet.

Facilities
Roadside parking, ski chalet, out-houses. A large trail map is posted at the trailhead, but you can request a map from the park by mail or fax, or visit www.pec.on.cawinterski.html.

Rentals
None.

Tips
Due to the lake influence, the area gets a lot of snow but loses it fast; so visit immediately after a snowfall. For accommodation, consider any one of the more than 100 bed and breakfast establishments on Quinte's Isle.

Cautions
Stay off the ice along the shoreline.

Tourism Info
Prince Edward County Tourism, 800-640-4717.

More Info
Sandbanks Provincial Park, 613-393-3319.

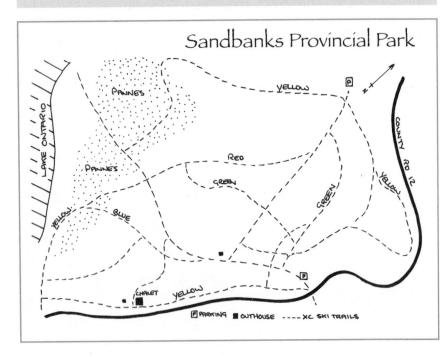

Sandbanks Provincial Park

P PARKING ■ OUTHOUSE ----- XC SKI TRAILS

47   FRINK CENTRE
North of Belleville

❊ hike through different ecosystems
❊ spy on deer
❊ see a variety of animal tracks

EVENTS
🙿 Winter Open House: First Sun in Feb
🙿 Guided Hikes: Fourth Sun of each month at 1 pm
🙿 Workshops: Monthly

Highlights: A river, a drumlin, erratics among cedars, a boardwalk through marsh
Impression: Remarkably diverse

Ever-Changing Ecosystems

Go north. Tread quietly beside the silver maple swamp on the chance of spotting deer at a maintained feeding station. Cross a bridge, and either follow a loop around a long drumlin that tapers smoothly at one end, or beeline up and over its aspen-covered hump, down to the Moira River, and hike along its tree-lined bank.

Alternatively, go south. Cross a beaver pond on a 500-metre-long boardwalk to a forest of cedars interspersed with erratics—huge rocks, displaced from the ice age. Or follow the Boundary Trail among horsetails and cattails, across bridges over icy streams, through frozen fields and wetlands.

Whichever the way, whatever the trail, the H. R. Frink Centre will have you roaming from one habitat to another. Diversity is the hallmark of this 400-acre conservation area owned by Quinte Conservation. Its 13 kilometres of well-marked, mapped and colour-coded loops, some narrow, others wide, lead through numerous different ecosystems.

Site of an outdoor education and natural science learning facility run by the Hastings and Prince Edward District School Board, trails are heavily used by school groups and tend to get hard-packed. Snowshoes are generally not required, though the south end gets less trampled than the north.

Friends of the Frink Centre, a volunteer group that built the boardwalk, among other projects, presents monthly workshops and guided hikes, as well as an annual Winter Open House, featuring outdoor cooking skills, winter survival techniques, bird and animal track identification, and naturalist-led snowshoe treks.

GUIDE NOTES

Location
9 km north of Belleville. From Hwy 401, take Hwy 37 north 9 km to Thrasher Rd, turn right and go 2 km. There's a small parking lot on the road's south side and portable classrooms on the north. Trails are on both sides of the road, free trail maps are at the trailheads.

Open
Daily.

Cost
Free.

Facilities
Outhouses.

Events/Programs
Winter Open House, $2 adults, $1 children, $5 families. Guided hikes are free, but donations appreciated. Workshops $20. Annual membership to Friends of the Frink Centre, $5 adults, $2 student, $10 families.

Tourism Info
Getaway Country, 800-461-1912, 613-332-1513, fax 613-332-2119, chamber@commerce.bancroft.on.ca, www.commerce.bancroft.on.ca.

More Info
Frink Centre, 613-477-2828, www.hcbe.edu.on.ca/coll/frink.htm or Quinte Conservation, 613-968-3434, www.pec.on.ca/conservation/.

Frink Centre

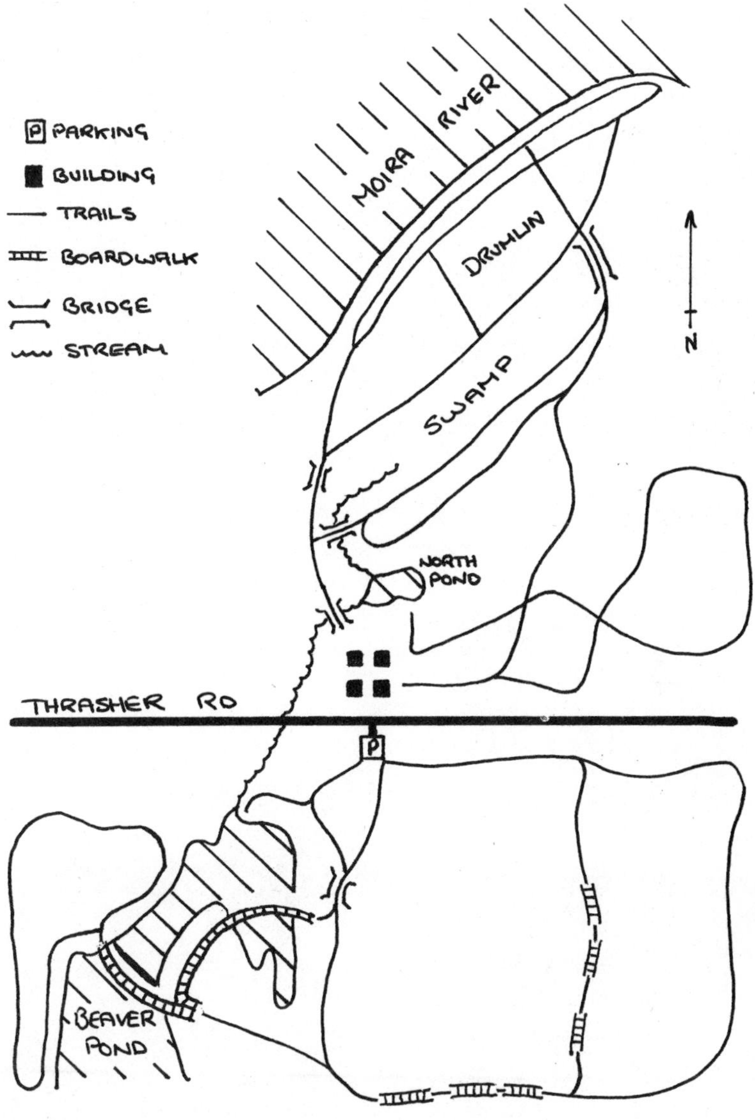

P PARKING
■ BUILDING
— TRAILS
≡ BOARDWALK
⊔ BRIDGE
〜 STREAM

MOIRA RIVER

DRUMLIN

SWAMP

NORTH POND

N

THRASHER RD

P

BEAVER POND

KINGSTON

48 LITTLE CATARAQUI CREEK CONSERVATION AREA
North of Kingston

❅ cross-country ski
❅ snowshoe
❅ skate
❅ hike

EVENTS
🐚 Interpretive programs: Most Sun
🐚 Maple Madness: Mid-March to early April
🐚 Valentine Evening Skate: Mid-Feb
🐚 Moonlight Ski and Skate: Early March

Highlights: Interpretive programs, skiing through diverse terrain, Friday-night skating
Impression: A delightful user-friendly winter playground

Snow Wonder
Bulrushes and pussy willows surround a Y-shaped reservoir in the heart of Little Cataraqui Creek Conservation Area, where a long, cleared skating area is lit on Friday nights. Groomed trails for cross-country skiing—13 kilome-

SUE LEBRECHT

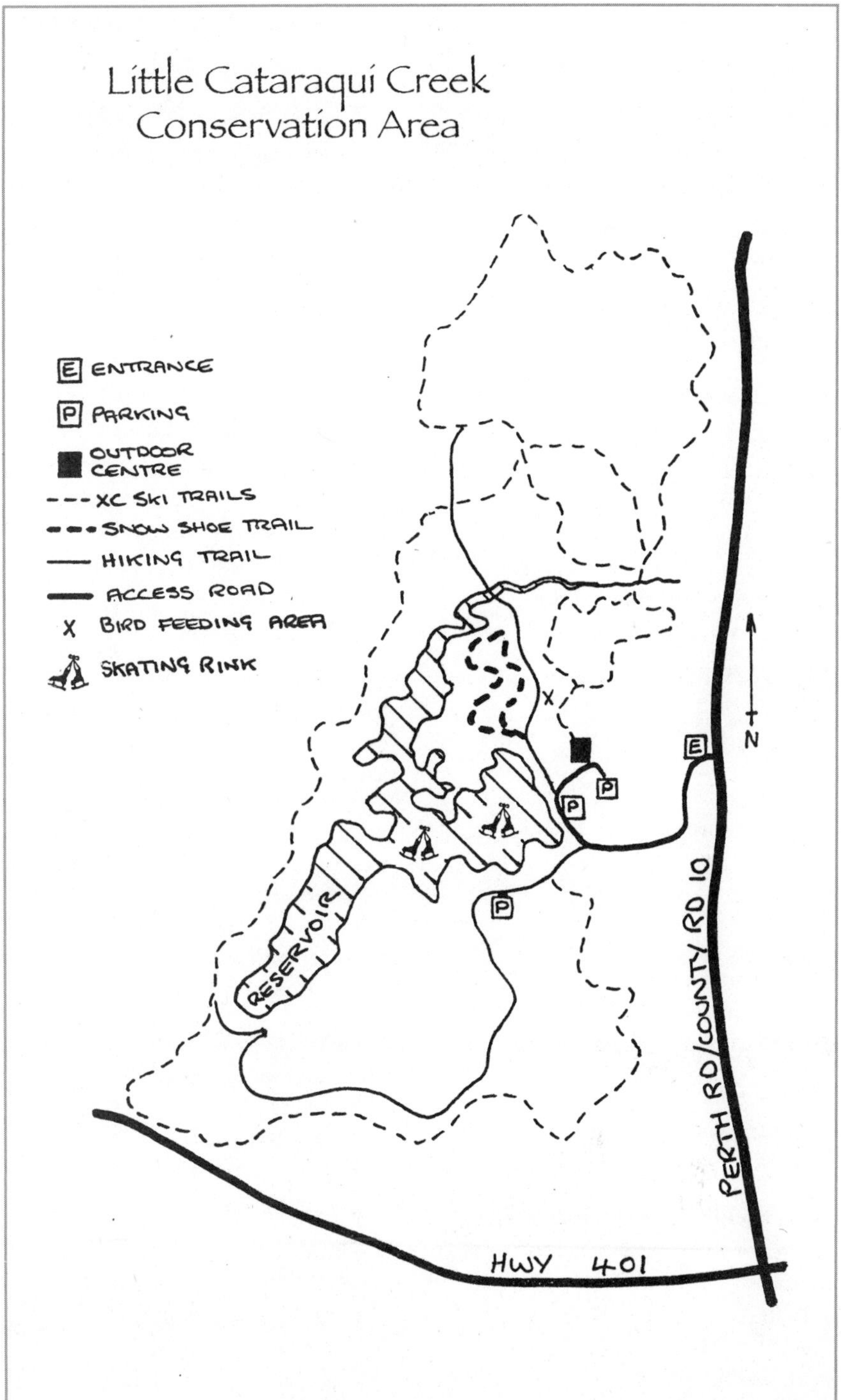

Little Cataraqui Creek Conservation Area

E ENTRANCE

P PARKING

■ OUTDOOR CENTRE

- - - XC SKI TRAILS

●●● SNOW SHOE TRAIL

— HIKING TRAIL

━ ACCESS ROAD

X BIRD FEEDING AREA

SKATING RINK

X

E

P

P

P

RESERVOIR

N

PERTH RD/COUNTY RD 10

HWY 401

tres worth—loop around it and beyond, into the northern reaches, among open fields, pine forest and sugar bush.

At one end of the reservoir, an Outdoor Centre with a snack bar, gift shop and observation deck welcomes visitors. It offers cross-country ski, snowshoe and skate rentals, and presents special programs most Sundays, and a Maple Madness Festival in early spring. From it, a one-kilometre-long ungroomed snowshoe trail loops to the creek that feeds the reservoir, a boardwalk leads to a bird-feeding area, and two service roads that are closed to vehicles but hard packed and open to hiking beeline north and southwest.

A busy playground, the park also offers cross-country ski lessons on Saturdays, a variety of weekday seniors' programs, and provides rink-side warming huts and Friday-night bonfires.

Sunday programs include a Natural Christmas Celebration; ski waxing, winter camping and snowshoe clinics; a birding slide show and hike; a ski loppet; and a sugar-bush maintenance workshop. During Maple Madness, tractor-drawn wagons provide rides to the sugar bush, where interpretive displays and hot pancakes with maple syrup await, while puppet shows are held in the Outdoor Centre.

GUIDE NOTES

Location
From Hwy 401 in Kingston, take Exit 617 and go north 2 km on Perth Rd (County Rd 10). Entrance is on your left.

Open
The Outdoor Centre is open weekdays 8:30 am to 4:30 pm, and weekends 9 am to 5 pm. Friday-night skating is offered Jan and Feb, 5 to 9 pm.

Cost
$6 per vehicle.

Facilities
The Outdoor Centre has a snack bar, gift shop and observation deck.

Rentals
Cross-country skis and snowshoes are available.

Programs
Cross-country ski lessons are offered Sat at 11 am and 1 pm, Jan and Feb for $10 per person; register at the Outdoor Centre on the day of the lesson. For children, a series of four lessons is offered for $30. Maple Madness takes place weekends from mid-March to early April and weekdays during March Break.

Tourism Info
Kingston Visitor Centre, 613-548-4415, www.kingstoncanada.com.

More Info
Cataraqui Region Conservation Authority, 613-546-4228, interpretive programs ext 500, rink conditions ext 501, cross-country ski lessons and rentals ext 222 or ext 232.

49 FRONTENAC PROVINCIAL PARK
North of Kingston

* backcountry ski
* snowshoe
* winter camp
* learn to winter camp
* cross-country ski

Highlights: Trekking through deep, untracked snow, winter camping
Impression: Real adventure, white oasis

Out There
You come to trek through deep snow, breaking trail on skis or snowshoes, following marked routes on trees. You come to winter camp, experience solitude and be challenged. Frontenac Provincial Park offers the wilderness. Within its extensive 160-kilometre trail network, only 13 kilometres are trackset for cross-country skiing. The rest, marked on trees, are untracked and untouched.

FRONTENAC PROVINCIAL PARK

Sound inviting? Those without experience in winter backcountry pursuits can learn how, in a winter camping course offered by the Friends of Frontenac. A one-day trip-planning presentation in late January is followed by two separate instructional weekend trips in February.

The planning presentation—a prerequisite to the instructional outings—covers equipment, menu, route selection, low-impact camping, safety, and different forms of winter travel. The instructional weekends introduce participants to snow houses, meal preparation, use of a map and compass, staying warm and other general winter camping skills.

Those already equipped with experience and knowledge have a haven at their feet. The park's south end is extremely rugged, with scattered coniferous trees, bare outcrops and extensive rock ridges affording long vistas. The north end, laced with lakes and a granite section of the Canadian Shield, presents a rolling lowland of dense deciduous forest, with two gorges, numerous beaver swamps and meadows. Interconnected loops roam the gamut, and staff at the Trail Centre can help you choose a route to match your ability.

Camp sites, each with a picnic table and firepit, are spread out in 13 different lakeside clusters, each with an outhouse and emergency supply barrel. But you needn't rough it outdoors overnight. Within a 30-minute drive of the park are more than half-a-dozen bed-and-breakfast establishments, and numerous cottage and cabin rentals.

GUIDE NOTES

Location
North of Kingston, off Hwy 38, 15 km north of Sydenham.

Open
Daily. Trail Centre is occasionally staffed on weekends, 8:30 am to 4:30 pm.

Cost
$7.50/vehicle per day. Camping $8 adults, $3.75 youths; permits required, available at the Trail Centre.

Facilities
Trail Centre, 48 campsites in 13 clusters equipped with an outhouse and emergency supply barrel.

Rentals
None.

Programs
Winter Camping Instructional Weekend Trip, $50 per person plus interior camping fee; food provided.

Tips
Make advance camping reservations. Call for snow conditions before heading out.

Cautions
Some trails include steep ravines and narrow cliffs. Always tell somebody where you're going and for how long. Use the buddy system. Never cross lakes or creeks without testing ice surfaces. Areas near creek mouths can be unsafe, even during the coldest weather. Carry a piece of wire or nylon cord to repair poles or bindings.

Tourism Info
The park has a listing of nearby bed and breakfasts and other lodging options. Ontario East Tourism, 800-567-3278 or 613-269-3999, fax 613-269-4885, onteast@magma.ca, www.ontarioeast.com.

More Info
Frontenac Provincial Park, 613-376-3489, reservations 888-668-7275, www.ontarioparks.com.

FRONTENAC PROVINCIAL PARK

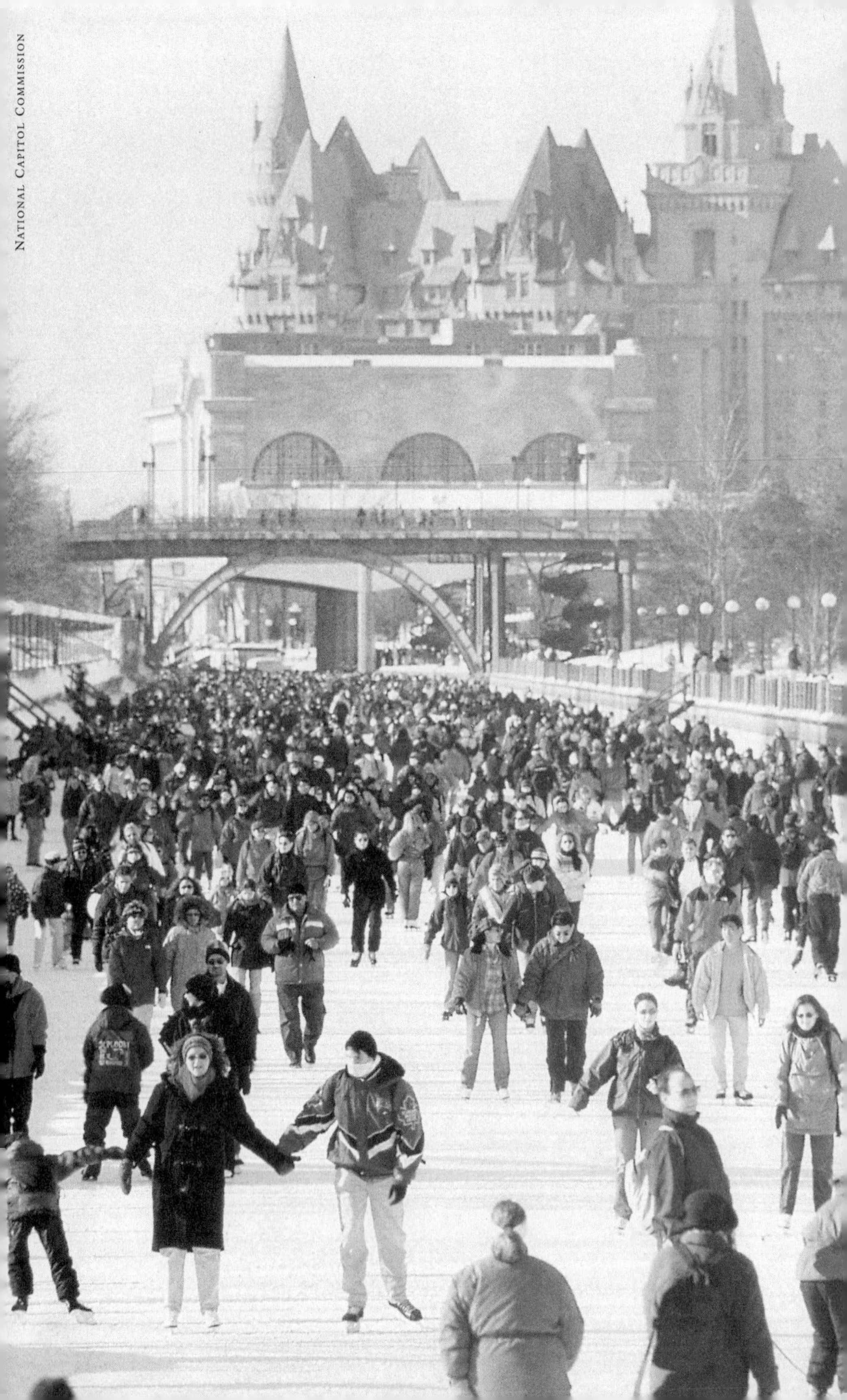

National Capitol Commission

OTTAWA

50 *WINTERLUDE*
Ottawa

* skate on a canal
* see snow sculptures and ice carvings
* watch figure-skating shows and zany ice performances
* see fireworks
* ride horse-drawn sleighs

When: First three weekends in Feb
Highlights: Skating on the world's largest outdoor rink, enjoying Snowflake Kingdom with your children
Impression: After experiencing this big outdoor party you'll never want to skate in circles again

Capital Canal

The Rideau Canal, the world's longest ice rink, serves as the main stage for Winterlude, North America's largest winter festival. From Dow's Lake to the National Arts Centre, through the heart of the National Capital, the snow-cleared, 7.8-kilometre-long promenade is site of the opening ceremonies, featuring a fireworks display. It's host to figure-skating shows, the annual Bed Race, the Buskers on Ice show, a relay, and hockey shoot-out. Ice-carving and snow-sculpting competitions take place on its banks. And for those who come to skate on it, concessionaires offer rink-side rentals, sharpening, hot drinks and snacks.

But the extravaganza of Winterlude, attracting more than 600,000 visitors, extends beyond the canal. In Jacques Cartier Park, Snowflake Kingdom provides kids with giant snowslides, craft workshops, dog sledding and horse-drawn sleigh rides. Queen Juliana Park is host to a hot air balloon fiesta. Gatineau Park features the Keskinada Loppet, an international cross-country competition that attracts an average of 2,000 competitors from more than 20 countries. At numerous indoor venues, event-goers can see art exhibits, dance troupes, musical performances and films.

A festival program provides event dates, locations, accommodation information and city maps.

PIERRE ST. JACQUES

GUIDE NOTES

Location
The festival takes place throughout the Capital region.

Cost
Most activities are free.

Tips
Book lodging months in advance. Also, see page 165 on Gatineau Park.

Tourism Info
Ottawa Tourism, 613-237-5150, www.tourottawa.org.

More Info
National Capital Commission, 800-465-1867, www.capcan.ca.

51   GATINEAU PARK
North of Ottawa

* cross-country ski
* skate-ski
* backcountry ski
* snowshoe
* hike hard-packed trails
* stay overnight in trail-side cabins and yurts
* winter camp
* alpine ski, snowboard
* dog sled

Highlight: Skiing in a lofty forest and lodging in a rustic cabin
Impression: One of Canada's premier cross-country ski destinations.

Adventure Mecca
Located 20 minutes north of the National Capital, in Quebec, Gatineau Park features 150 kilometres of well-maintained, double-tracked cross-country ski trails, 80 kilometres of groomed skate-skiing lanes and 50 kilometres of ungroomed backcountry ski routes. Scattered throughout the network are eight day-use shelters with picnic tables, wood-burning stoves and safety radio systems.

A handful of cabins and yurts in the northern region offer rustic overnight options. For adventurers, there are remote camping sites, and for those who prefer hot showers, heat, electricity and kitchen facilities at the end of the day, the Carman Trails Youth Hostel, and Camp Gatineau, an outdoor centre, offer bunk accommodation right on the trail system.

The network, accessible from 14 different parking lots, is well marked, mapped and colour-coded with ratings for different skill levels. Trails loop and link for extensive meandering around a mosaic of frozen lakes and forested hills, with ridges, cliffs, rocky outcrops, boulders, creeks and ponds.

For the most part the terrain rolls, presenting both steep ascents and long gradual climbs. Trail 1, for example, rises 100 metres over less than 500 metres. Trail 52 has a continuous climb for 6 kilometres, but heading northwards, towards Wakefield, that stretch translates to one long downhill.

There are two flat trails, however. The 4-kilometre North Loop, near the Visitors' Centre (from parking lot 8), is ideal for families and beginners. Trail 50 from Lac Philippe (parking lot 19) to the Herridge Shelter, a farmhouse built in 1880, offers a 10-kilometre, long and level, one-way journey.

Pick and choose. There are wide boulevards, winding, undulating tracks and narrow, up-and-down bush trails. Trail 1, which leads past three shelters up to Champlain Lookout, forms a spine, with branching trails along its length. From it, the narrow, ungroomed expert-rated Trail 6, also called the Skyline, leads up to a view over the city of Ottawa. From Meech Lake (parking lot 12), the intermediate/expert-rated Trail 2 involves a steep, 2-kilometre-long climb to the Western Shelter, which sits on the edge of a 300-metre-high escarpment, with a vista of the Ottawa River Valley.

Way Out Snoozing

Opting for an overnight? Start at Parking Lot 11 and ski the easy/intermediate-rated trails 36, 50 and 52 for a 25-kilometre, one-way excursion to the Brown Lake Cabin or beyond to Wakefield. The quaint village of Wakefield, adjacent to the park in the north, and the village of Old Chelsea in the south, both offer a number of bed-and-breakfast establishments.

The Brown Lake Cabin sleeps 16 and is the only cabin with electricity, a fridge and stove. Three other cabins plus two yurts sleep 6 to 8 guests and are simply equipped with bunkbeds, mattresses and wood stoves. Located in relatively close proximity to each other, they are not suited for hut-to-hut-style skiing, but rather as a home base for daytrips in the surrounding area. A couple are located on backcountry trails, while the others are accessible on groomed, trackset intermediate trails. And if you're not with a group, you'll be sharing a roof with strangers.

Guests are required to bring their own water, light source, cooking burner, utensils and sleeping bag. But you needn't carry all that gear; the park offers luggage services and will deliver your stuff to a cabin or yurt for a fee.

Gatineau Park also has 20 kilometres of dedicated snowshoe trails and 12 kilometres of hard-packed winter hiking trails. For snowshoeing, there are three circuits in the Lac Philippe area. For hiking, four loops in the southern region—one of which leads to the ruins of the Mackenzie King Estate—range between 2 and 4 kilometres.

The park is also home to Camp Fortune, an alpine resort with a healthy vertical drop of 195 metres, 17 trails and 5 lifts.

GUIDE NOTES

Location
From Hwy 417, exit Nicholas and follow signs to Hull/King Edward St N, go across the MacDonald/ Cartier Bridge and follow Hwy 5 approximately 10 km to Old Chelsea (Exit 12). Turn left at the stop sign and follow Old Chelsea/Meech Rd for 2 km to the Visitors' Centre on your right.

Open
Daily.

Cost
Ski fees (which include parking) are $8 adults, seniors $5, families $18. Cabin and yurt lodging fees range from $15 to $18 per person per night. Overnight fees at Camp Gatineau, 819-456-2002, are $35, and at Carman Trails Youth Hostel 819-459-3180, www.magma.ca/~carman, which has its own 12 km network of cross-country ski trails and 8 km of snowshoe trails with rentals, fees are $16 for members and $20 for non-members.

Facilities
The Visitors' Centre has trail maps, route suggestions, washrooms. Cabin and yurt reservations are also made here.

Rentals
Snowshoes are available from the Visitors' Centre. Cross-country ski rentals are available at Greg Christie's Ski & Cycle Works, 819-827-5340, and Gerry and Isobel's, 819-827-4341 in Old Chelsea near the park's eastern boundary.

Events/Programs
Dog sledding in the Gatineau Hills is offered by Expéditions Radisson, 819-459-3860.

Tips
Book early for cabins and yurt rentals. To get to Ottawa, consider travelling Via Rail, 416-366-8411, www.viarail.ca. Back Country Bus, a transportation service, offers pickup from major hotels and bus and train stations in Ottawa to various trail-heads in the park, including the one at the Carman Youth Hostel near Wakefield, and to Camp Fortune. Return cost ranges from $16 to $22, 613-851-7045 or 819-459-3180, www.magma.ca/~carman/bus.htm

Tourism Info
Ottawa Tourism, 613-237-5150, www.tourottawa.org.

More Info
Gatineau Park Visitor Centre, 819-827-2020, gpvisito@ncc-ccn.ca or the National Capital Commission, 800-465-1867, www.capcan.ca Camp Fortune, 819-827-1717, www.campfortune.com.